Something More Than Burgers 'n Fries

GUILT·FREE Fast Foods

Recipes for nutritious foods you can cook in less than an hour...

Yvonne G. Baker

ACCENT BOOKS
Denver, Colorado

ACCENT BOOKS

A division of Accent Publications, Inc.
12100 W. Sixth Avenue
P.O. Box 15337
Denver, Colorado 80215

Library of Congress Catalog Card Number 84-070428
ISBN 0-89636-129-2

First Printing 1984
Second Printing 1984

Guilt Free Fast Foods

In appreciation for your support of Focus on the Family, please accept this copy of *Guilt Free Fast Foods* by Yvonne Baker. Your contributions enable this organization to address the needs of homes through radio, television, literature and counseling.

We trust Yvonne Baker's creative recipes for quick, nutritious meals will be enjoyed by you and your family. This cookbook will make a fine addition to your kitchen library.

Focus on the Family
P.O. Box 500
Arcadia, CA 91006

ACKNOWLEDGMENTS

This book could not have been written without the support and love of a very special group of people—the Dale House.

The Dale House is a project that reaches out to troubled, runaway or homeless teenagers. At the Dale House they receive a place to sleep, food, counseling and friendship. Some kids are only there for a night, some for several years.

In addition to the work with kids, the Dale House is also, in part, a training program for graduate students who wish to spend a year in combining academic study with practical experience in ministry to troubled youth.

Several years ago I began cooking at the Dale House as a volunteer. This year my book project has become a group project. The recipes in this book were cooked together, tested and commented upon by the entire community—kids and staff. From group meals of 20-40 people to little dinners at my house, the Dale House community gave me help and encouragement while developing and writing the recipes, and exhibited lots of courage and good humor in eating my new experiments.

They also gave me laughter and excitement when I was depressed; love and acceptance at a time in my life when I needed it so badly, and they did the dishes and cleaned up after the huge messes I made.

This book is for them and because of them, and without them it couldn't have been written.

Yvonne G. Baker

DEDICATION

To the
Dale House Staff
and Kids,
1983-1984

—the joy of my life—

CONTENTS

ABOUT THE AUTHOR. . .

YVONNE G. BAKER lives in Colorado Springs, Colorado, though her speaking appearances and natural foods classes extend beyond Colorado to other parts of the country. She is a foods columnist for the *Colorado Springs Sun*, and teaches numerous cooking classes.

"Food that is healthful and well-prepared is very important to me," says Yvonne. "It's one of our most basic and continuing needs and one of my favorite ways of tangibly showing love to people around me."

Her three previously published books are:

FROM GOD'S NATURAL STOREHOUSE
THE HOLIDAY COOKBOOK—How To Celebrate with
         Wholesome, Natural Foods
GUILT-FREE SNACKING.

NEVER ENOUGH TIME

"I'm late, I'm late for a very important date! No time to lose, no time to waste, I'm late, I'm late, I'm late!"

So often our lives echo these lines from *Alice in Wonderland.* We've got so much to do, we're running late, and we certainly don't have time to stop and cook a big meal.

But we have to eat. Our bodies are so bothersome. Three times a day they demand food. If we don't answer that demand we get weak or grouchy, and if we try to ignore the demand often enough, we get sick.

So we grab something fast. A donut for breakfast, a burger and a coke for lunch, maybe fast food fried chicken or a TV dinner at night. But then we feel guilty. We feel like we've been eating cardboard decorated to look like food and our bodies tell us that we might as well have eaten cardboard for all the nutrition we received from a diet like that. But we don't know what else to do. We really think that cooking nutritiously takes a long time and is difficult. So day after day we go on feeling guilty about how we eat and how we feed our families, convinced that there isn't anything we can do about it.

FAST FOOD AT HOME

I used to feel that way. My friends felt like that. People who read what I wrote about healthful food constantly said, "Your ideas sound good, but I just don't have the time."

"Who does?" I was starting to ask as my life got more and more frantic.

"Write a cookbook for me—for someone who has to make dinner quickly after taking care of two preschoolers all day."

"I need healthful things I can prepare after dashing in the door at 6:00 p.m. and my feet hurt."

"I'm a student. I can't spend all day in the kitchen, but I want to eat better. Help me!"

More and more the requests came for food that was healthy, but food that was fast and easy to make.

So I started thinking. By the time you take off to go somewhere for fast foods, drive there, stand in line, eat and get back to wherever, you've usually used up about one hour. Even a TV dinner takes about that long to get out, heat up and eat. I wondered, could you make a healthful meal at home in less than an hour? Could something be convenient and not come out of a box? Even more important, could it be convenient and good for you at the same time?

Those were the challenges of this book: food that would be healthy, *and* prepared in under an hour.

THE RESULT

It worked! And it worked well.

It is amazing, the wonderful things you can do with food in less than an hour. You alter certain things, like sizes. Make little meatloaves in muffin tins, and slice up vegetables you used to bake whole. Make breads that are quick rising and salads that are simple. You skip some complicated steps that just made recipes harder anyway, and you learn a multitude of delicious sauces that turn the simplest of foods, sauteed golden chicken breasts for example, into gourmet treats.

Everything in this cookbook can be made in less than an hour. You can combine a number of dishes and still have a whole meal ready in under an hour. Depending upon how experienced a cook you are and how organized your kitchen is, the time may vary slightly. Or, if you are using a very dull knife and don't know how to chop onions too well, the time may increase a bit, but no matter what, these recipes will go faster than most.

Best of all, you don't need any special equipment to make these things in under an hour. You don't have to remember to put things in a crockpot, or do things ahead to save time later. Though there are many helpful time-saving appliances, I wanted this cookbook to be useful to anyone.

A NOTE ON INGREDIENTS

For the recipes to be of maximum value, it is important that you use the most healthful ingredients.

The recipes call for basically healthful ingredients such as whole wheat flour and honey. But there are many cases where you will have to choose certain items. When oil is called for, use a good safflower or other unsaturated oil without preservatives. Read labels and get a product with as few refined products, sugar, chemicals and preservatives in it as possible.

When using the recipes feel free to alter ingredients if your diet and taste require it. You can always cut down on sweetner. You can cut salt down or out completely. These ingredients are for flavor only and may be modified if you wish.

Speaking of altering recipes, if you like to do that—feel free. I had fun experimenting with these. You can, too. If you feel like cheddar cheese instead of jack, don't run to the store to buy exactly what I called for—create your own taste treat. Cooking is much more enjoyable if we don't feel we're held captive by the exactness of a recipe.

A NOTE ABOUT FOOD CODING

None of us have time to look up the calorie, or protein or fiber content of the recipes we are preparing, but often we know we want to modify our diet in certain areas. The following symbols will help you quickly spot the following food categories.

LOW CALORIE: the calorie content per serving in this category is under 200 calories.

HIGH PROTEIN: the protein content per serving in this category is over 5 grams of protein. In most of the main meat dishes it is quite a bit higher where this is indicated.

UNSATURATED OILS: for individuals who wish to avoid saturated fats (butter, margarine, etc.) these recipes contain only unsaturated oils.

HIGH FIBER: foods marked with this symbol are especially high in fiber. This is one of the most important needs in our modern diets which contain so many highly refined foods. Digestive problems, constipation, various forms of cancer, and weight problems have all been shown to be helped or avoided by increased fiber intake.

A FINAL INTRODUCTORY NOTE

We all want to give to the people we love. But we can't all give equally. We may be rich or poor, talented or handicapped, powerful or weak, and we feel limited in our ability to give as we wish we could.

But we all have an equal amount of one thing—time. God did not give some people 36 hour days and other people 10 hour days. We're all equal with that resource. We decide how to spend it.

I believe the most important gift we can ever give someone is time—undivided, focused and caring. Writing a book telling you how to save time in the kitchen is not meant to devalue the joy of cooking. Hopefully, rather, it will free up a little more of that precious commodity—time. Please give away the moments you save in love.

APPETIZERS
AND
PARTY FOODS

"Let your speech be alway with grace, seasoned with salt, that ye may know how ye ought to answer every man."
—Colossians 4:6

APPETIZERS
AND
PARTY FOODS

Appetizers and party foods—of all the catagories of food that you want to be able to prepare quickly, these top the list.

You want to be able to spend your time with your guests, not in the kitchen. So anything that saves time for you is bound to make your entertaining more pleasant. A variety of the foods below will make a party. One or two of them is the perfect beginning to any meal.

I strongly suggest an appetizer before beginning any meal for guests. I have always found it rather unnerving to be immediately hustled to the table after coming in the door. One always has the uncomfortable suspicion that you were keeping everyone from their meal. An appetizer time allows the cook to put the last minute touches on the meal and gives everyone time to relax, to talk and to enjoy one another before sitting down to eat. Your appetizers need not be elaborate. One or two of the following recipes in this section is sufficient for any meal. Iced herb teas are very nice to serve with appetizers as are fruit juices mixed with club soda or mineral water.

If you are caught with unexpected guests and no time to prepare some of the formal recipes, try any of these SUPER QUICK APPETIZER IDEAS.

SUPER QUICK APPETIZER IDEAS

— peanut butter in celery sticks
— mixed nuts and sunflower seeds
— carrot slices and orange wedges
— popcorn with seasoning salt tossed in
— any sort of cheese and crackers. An apple or two is nice alongside.
— breadsticks
— corn tortillas with cheese melted on top
— leftover quiche cut into little squares
— any sort of sandwich filling. Put it on crackers, top with a bit of pickle, and it looks special.
— cheese on crackers with a dab of hot pepper jelly or chutney on top

Antipasto

In the world of Italian cooking antipasto literally means the course that "comes before the pasta." Antipasto can be made from an incredible assortment of foods: sliced cheese, tuna, olives, fresh vegetables, marinated mushrooms, etc., all sprinkled with a tangy vinegar and oil dressing.

And it couldn't be easier. You don't have to cook a thing. You simply place the foods you have selected on a plate of lettuce and pour the dressing over. It's almost as easy as popping popcorn for guests.

1 head leaf lettuce,
  cleaned
1 6½ oz. can water
  packed tuna,
  drained
6 thin slices
  monterey jack
  cheese
6 thin slices
  mozzarella cheese
12 cherry tomatoes
6 green onions,
  cleaned and
  trimmed
1 cucumber, sliced
12 fresh mushrooms,
  cleaned and cut in
  half
12 black olives

Dressing:
⅔ cup olive oil
⅓ cup vinegar
1 tsp. dried basil
¼ tsp. garlic powder
  dash salt
  dash pepper

On a large platter place the lettuce leaves. Arrange each ingredient in sections, forming an attractive pattern. Combine the dressing ingredients. Pour dressing over the platter. Cover the platter with plastic wrap. It can be served immediately, or it can be refrigerated for up to four hours before serving.
Serves 6-8 for an appetizer, 4 for a light main dish.

VARIATIONS:
Greek antipasto: instead of mozzarella and jack cheese, use feta. Also, add one can of marinated artichoke hearts. In the dressing omit the basil and add ½ teaspoon oregano and dash of dried mint.
Vegetarian antipasto: omit the meat and cheese. Use one large bag of frozen mixed vegetables (the ones cut in large pieces). Run under cold water until thawed. Add additional fresh vegetables, if desired, but if in a hurry this will do. Proceed as above.
Miscellaneous variations: antipasto can be made from any assortment of vegetables, leftovers, canned meats or whatever. In addition to some of the ingredients listed, you can use canned salmon, cold bits of chicken or turkey, any variety of pickles or pickled vegetables. Let your imagination be your guide.

Miscellaneous Notes:
— Antipasto is delicious served with French bread or bread sticks.
— Served with bread and a beverage, a large platter of antipasto makes a complete meal.
— Small individual antipastos can be arranged on individual plates for a more formal appetizer.
— Tossed together, the leftovers make a great salad.

Brie with Almonds

A poem of the fifteenth century compared brie with gold for its richness and value. It really is a wonderful cheese. Allowed to come to room temperature and served by itself it makes a delicious appetizer. The following recipes make it even more special.

1 small round brie
2 T. sliced almonds
1 T. butter
dash nutmeg

Place brie on a pie plate in a preheated 325° oven. Heat for about 10 minutes. While brie is heating, melt the butter in a small skillet. Add the sliced almonds and dash of nutmeg. Cook for about 7 minutes. Remove brie from oven, place on a serving platter and spoon toasted almonds over. Serve with plain crackers and a knife to cut the cheese.
Serves 4.

Brie with Pesto

1 small round brie
¼ cup pesto, either the frozen kind from a deli or from the recipe on page 118.
¼ cup pine nuts

Place the brie on a pie plate in a preheated 325° oven. Heat for about 10 minutes. While brie is heating, place the pesto and the pine nuts in a small skillet. Stir gently over low heat for about five minutes, or until heated through. Remove brie from oven, place on a serving platter and spoon the heated pesto and pine nuts over. Serve with plain crackers.
Serves 4.

Escargot in Mushroom Caps

Long thought of as a gourmet dish, snails or escargot have been eaten as a favorite appetizer since Roman times. Since they are available canned in most grocery stores, it takes only minutes to make the exotic appetizer below.

1 **small can snails**
1 **cup beef broth**
½ **bay leaf**
1 **clove garlic**
¾ **cup butter,**
   softened
2 **T. green onion,**
   very finely minced
2 **cloves garlic, very**
   finely minced
1 **T. parsley, finely**
   minced
   dash salt and
   pepper
16 **or more large,**
   fresh mushrooms

Remove snails from can and rinse several times. In a small skillet place the snails, beef broth, ½ bay leaf and clove of garlic. Simmer gently for about 10 minutes. While snails are simmering, combine the butter, green onion, garlic and parsley. If you have a food processor or blender, just chop the green onion, garlic and parsley in it and then add the butter. Clean the mushrooms and remove the stems. Place the mushrooms in a shallow baking dish. Remove snails from simmering broth and place in mushroom caps. If the snails are very large they can be cut in half. Place a dab of the butter mixture on top of each snail filled mushroom. Heat in a 350° oven for about 10 minutes or until heated through. Serve immediately.

Serves 4-6.

VEGETABLES AND DIPS

Vegetables and dips are a perennial favorite as an appetizer and party food. Vegetables supply vitamins, minerals and necessary fiber for the diet. Unfortunately, all of this goodness is often diminished by the use of commercial, chemical dips served with the vegetables. Instead, try some of the delicious and healthful dips that follow. You can choose low calorie, high protein, mild or spicy. Whatever you choose, you can never go wrong serving vegetables and dips as a party or snack food.

Chili Con Queso

This tangy, hot dip can be kept in a chafing or other warmed dish and tortilla chips can be dipped into it, or you can make it up and pour it over a platter of chips—a little messier to eat, but still yummy.

1 8 oz. can tomatoes, pureed first
1 4 oz. can chili peppers, chopped, as hot or as mild as you prefer
3 green onions, chopped
½ tsp. garlic powder
½ tsp. powdered cumin
2½ cups grated cheddar cheese
2½ cups grated jack cheese

In a medium size saucepan place the pureed tomatoes, chili peppers, green onions, cumin and garlic powder. Stir together over medium heat until combined and heated through. Gradually add cheese and stir until cheese melts. You may have to turn up the heat, but don't allow mixture to boil. When all is combined, either pour over tortilla chips or place in a heated dish and dip chips into it.

Makes about 4 cups.

Creamy Clam Dip

This is a very refreshing and delicious dip. The clams add protein and their own distinctive flavor.

1 cup plain yogurt
1 can minced clams, drained well
1 small tomato, finely chopped
½ cucumber, peeled, seeded and finely chopped
1 green onion, finely chopped
dash salt and pepper

Gently stir together all ingredients and serve.

Makes about 2 cups.

Tapenade

In addition to being a different and delicious dip for fresh vegetables, tapenade can also be used as a sauce over cold pork and beef. Try it over leftovers to make them into a special meal.

1 7 oz. can
  waterpacked tuna,
  drained
⅓ cup fresh or fresh-
  frozen lemon juice
1 2 oz. can flat
  anchovies, drained
¼ cup pickle relish
1 4 oz. can chopped
  black olives,
  drained
¼ cup olive oil
  dash black pepper

Place tuna, lemon juice, anchovies, pickle relish, and black olives in a food processor and blend well. Add olive oil slowly while the processor is running. Season to taste with black pepper.

Makes about 2 cups.

Hummus

Hummus is a dip of Middle Eastern origin that contains chick-peas or garbanzo beans as its main ingredient. Chick-peas are rich in calcium, potassium, sodium, iron, phosphorus, and protein. To make this recipe quickly, purchase the canned chick-peas. They are just as nutritious as the dried ones and you will save yourself hours of soaking and cooking.

1 16 oz. can chick-
  peas
⅓ cup fresh lemon
  juice
2 cloves garlic,
  finely chopped
½ cup sesame tahini
1 T. or more olive oil
1 T. olive oil
  chopped parsley

Mix chick-peas, garlic, tahini and 1 tablespoon of the olive oil in a blender or food processor, adding more oil if necessary to achieve a spreadable consistency. When ready to serve, dribble on the additional oil and garnish with the parsley. Traditionally hummus is served with quarters of pita bread. It is also good with fresh vegetables.

Makes about 2 cups.

COTTAGE CHEESE DIPS

Cottage cheese is an excellent source of protein with 31 grams of protein per cup. It is also low in calories with only 235 calories per cup. Using cottage cheese as a dip for vegetables, therefore, is an excellent idea for your health as well as being delicious. Try the variations below or make up some of your own combinations.

 ## Green Cheese Dip

1 cup cottage
  cheese
1 T. lemon juice
2 T. plain yogurt
2 T. chopped green
  onions
¼ cup fresh parsley,
  chopped
½ tsp. tarragon
  dash salt and
  pepper

Combine all ingredients in a food processor or blender until creamy and well blended. Makes about 1¼ cups.

Sweet Cheese Dip

1 cup cottage
  cheese
¼ cup chopped
  prunes
¼ cup chopped
  apricots

Combine all ingredients in a food processor or blender until creamy and well blended. Makes about 1½ cups.

Chili Cheese Dip

1 **cup cottage cheese**
2 **T. plain yogurt**
½ **tsp. garlic salt**
¼ **tsp. crushed cumin**
¼ **tsp. chili powder**

Combine all ingredients in a food processor or blender until creamy and well blended. Makes about 1 cup.

CHEESE SPREADS

Serve them out of a crock, or decorative bowl, or pile them in the middle of a platter and surround them with crackers or fruit. However you decide to serve them, cheese spreads are easy and quick to make and a sure hit as an appetizer. The cheese supplies needed protein as well as flavor.

Homemade Boursin

1 **3 oz. package cream cheese**
3 **T. butter, softened**
¼ **tsp. garlic powder**
1 **T. minced parsley**
¼ **tsp. lemon pepper**
   dash onion salt
   dash marjoram
   dash thyme

Cream together all ingredients or blend in a food processor. Serve with crackers. Makes about ¾ cup.

Tangy Cheese Spread

1 3 oz. package
   cream cheese
½ cup blue cheese,
   crumbled
¼ cup butter,
   softened
1 tsp. caraway
   seeds, crushed
1 T. grated onion
2 tsp. capers
1 tsp. mustard

Cream all ingredients together or combine in a food processor. Serve with crackers or black pumpernickle bread.
Makes about 1 cup.

Gorgonzola and Pine Nuts

Slightly rich, this appetizer is quite delicious. Serve it with some fresh grapes for an elegant beginning.

½ cup gorgonzola
   cheese, crumbled
2 T. pine nuts
1 8 inch length of
   French bread cut
   in half lengthwise
   and cut almost
   through into four
   slices. Or use 4
   whole wheat
   English muffin
   halves.

Sprinkle gorgonzola on the French bread or muffins. Top with the pine nuts. Place in a 350° oven for about 10 minutes or until the cheese just begins to melt. Serve immediately.
Serves 4.

BEEF

Time is a sacred trust.
"Now is the day of salvation."

BEEF

One of the quickest of meats to prepare is the old standby ground beef. You can fry it, bake it, broil it. You can combine it with numerous other ingredients and infinitely vary the taste. Another plus of ground beef is that it remains one of the most inexpensive beef items.

Also available in many markets today are the ground beef and soybean combinations. They are even more inexpensive than regular ground beef. They taste fine and the added soybean means less fat in the finished product, a definite plus for your health. In addition to the soybean in the ground beef, you can also stretch any kind of ground beef yourself by adding bread or cracker crumbs, grated carrots or potatoes. One half cup of additive per pound of ground meat is the suggested proportion.

Speedy Meatloaf

2 lbs. ground beef
1 egg
2 slices of whole
   wheat bread, torn
   into small pieces
½ onion, finely
   chopped
2 T. catsup
1 T. Worchestershire
   sauce
½ tsp. garlic salt
   dash salt and
   pepper

Sauce:
1 T. butter or
   margarine
½ onion, chopped
1 cup fresh
   mushrooms,
   chopped
1 cup beef bouillon
1 T. cornstarch
1 tsp. Worchester-
   shire sauce
   dash salt and
   pepper

If you're used to meatloaf taking an hour or more to bake, you may be wondering what could possibly be speedy about meatloaf. The secret is in how you shape it. In a big loaf, of course, it takes a long time to cook. Shaped in smaller sizes, it cooks very quickly with the same delicious taste.

Preheat oven to 350°. In a medium size bowl lightly combine all meatloaf ingredients. Shape into small balls the size of your muffin cups and place in muffin tin. Bake about 15-20 minutes or until done.

While the meatloaf is baking make the sauce. In a medium size saucepan over medium heat, melt the butter or margarine. Add the onion and saute until it begins to soften. Add the mushrooms and cook a few more minutes. Dissolve cornstarch in the bouillon and pour into pan. Add Worchestershire, salt and pepper, and cook, stirring constantly until thick.

When little meatloaves are done, pile on a platter, cover with sauce and serve.

Serves 4-6.

Individual Mushroom Meatloaves

meatloaf recipe as
above
1 T. butter or
margarine
1 green onion,
chopped
1 cup mushrooms,
sliced
optional: ¼ cup
catsup

Preheat oven to 350°. Prepare meatloaf mixture as described above. Shape into four little loaves and place in a 9 x 13 baking dish. Bake about 20 minutes or until done. While baking, melt the butter over medium heat in a small skillet on top of the stove. Add the green onions and the mushrooms and gently saute until the mushrooms are soft. If desired, add the catsup and heat through. When ready to serve, place the little loaves on a serving platter and spoon the hot sauce over them.
Serves 4.

BAKED BURGERS

Hamburgers are a favorite fast food, both when eating out and when eating at home. Burgers made at home have lots of advantages: they can be bigger, juicier and have a greater variety in flavorings. They also cost much less to prepare at home.

 ## Baked Mushroom Burgers

1½ lbs. ground beef
1 cup fresh
mushrooms, sliced
1 tsp. butter or
margarine
dash Worchester-
shire sauce
dash salt and
pepper

Preheat oven to 350°. In a medium size bowl combine the ground beef with one-half cup of the mushrooms. Shape into 6 patties and place in a baking dish. Bake about 20 minutes or to desired doneness. While cooking, melt the butter or margarine over medium heat in a small skillet. Saute the remaining mushrooms. Add a dash of Worchestershire sauce. You can either spoon this sauce over the mushroom burgers while they are still baking or wait until you take them out of the oven and spoon the sauce on just before serving.
Serves 6.

Baked Cheeseburgers

These are cheeseburgers with a yummy difference. The cheese is inside.

2 **lbs. ground beef**
2 **cups cheddar cheese, grated**
¼ **cup onion, very finely chopped**
optional: catsup

Preheat oven to 350°. Shape meat into 10 burgers. Then slice each one in half and flatten again into patty shape. On the top of each of 10 halves, place the cheese, being sure it is well within the edges of the meat. Sprinkle on a little bit of chopped onion. Replace the other half of the meat and press the edges together well. Place patties in a baking dish and bake 20 minutes or to desired doneness. If desired, the last 10 minutes or so of baking, spoon on a little catsup for a sauce and add a little additional grated cheese.

Serves 6-10.

Hawaiian Burgers

If you want to, you can briefly grill the pineapple slices before placing them on top of the ground beef patties.

2 **lbs. ground beef**
1 **16 oz. can pineapple rings**

Preheat oven to 350°. Shape meat into 10 burgers. Put burgers in a baking dish and place pineapple slices on top. Pour juice from can over all. Bake 20 minutes.

Serves 6-10.

MEXICAN DISHES

From south of the border we find lots of inspiration for quick cooking. Mexican food featuring beef, beans and tortillas can be the basis for many delicious and easy meals. Any of the dishes below can be the main course for a lunch or supper or you can combine several. Mexican food is also great to serve at a buffet.

Check your store for whole wheat flour tortillas. Many places carry them, and they are much better for you than the white flour tortillas.

 ## Hamburger Green Chili

Feel free to adjust the seasonings in this and any of the other Mexican dishes. The degree of hotness is completely up to you.

1 lb. ground beef
1 onion, chopped
2 cloves garlic, minced
1 4 oz. can peppers, chopped (These can be as hot as you like, either the mild chili peppers or the hot jalepenos.)
1 16 oz. can tomatoes, chopped and juice drained
½ tsp. cumin
1 tsp. chili powder
dash salt and pepper
8 flour tortillas, whole wheat if possible

Preheat oven to 375°. In a medium size skillet place the ground beef, chopped onion and garlic. Brown meat over medium heat. Drain off grease. Add the chili peppers, drained tomatoes, cumin, salt and pepper. Place a large spoonful of the green chili in the center of each tortilla. Roll up and place in a baking dish. Pour remaining sauce over. Heat in oven until heated through, about 10 minutes.

Serves 4.

Hamburger Green Chili with Beans

Green chili recipe
above
1 16 oz. can refried
beans

Follow recipe above, but place several spoonsful of refried beans into each tortilla before rolling up and placing in the oven.

Green Chili Stew

Green chili recipe
from above
Reserved juice
from the tomatoes
1 32 oz. can
tomatoes
1 16 oz. can V-8
juice
water

In a soup kettle make the green chili as directed above. Then add the tomatoes, first mashing them. Add the V-8 juice and heat through. Add water until soup is of desired consistency. Serve as a soup, with buttered flour tortillas.
Serves 4-6.

Beef and Bean Enchiladas

1 lb. ground beef
1 medium onion,
chopped
¼ tsp. garlic powder
¼ tsp. cumin
1 can refried beans
12 corn tortillas
2 8 oz. cans
enchilada sauce
2 cups cheddar
cheese, shredded
½ cup sour cream or
half sour cream,
half plain yogurt
1 4 oz. can black
olives, sliced

Preheat oven to 350°. In a medium size skillet saute the ground beef and the onion until the beef is done. Pour off excess grease. Add garlic powder, cumin and refried beans. Stir together. Place mixture into tortillas and roll up. Place in a 9 x 13 baking dish and cover with enchilada sauce. Place cheese on top. Bake uncovered about 15 minutes or until heated through. Remove from oven. Garnish with sour cream and olives and serve.
Serves 6.

Tacoritos

These are a favorite of mine because of the lettuce and tomatoes in them. I think it makes their taste less heavy.

1 lb. ground beef
1 T. chili powder
¼ tsp. garlic powder
½ tsp. cumin
2 T. chopped green chilis
1 cup grated cheddar cheese
2 tomatoes, chopped
½ head iceburg lettuce, shredded
12 flour tortillas, whole wheat if possible
1 8 oz. can enchilada sauce
1 cup cheddar cheese

Preheat oven to 350°. Place the ground beef in a large skillet and brown. Drain grease. Add chili powder, garlic powder, and cumin. Stir together well. Add green chilis, 1 cup of the grated cheddar cheese, the tomatoes, and iceburg lettuce. Stir together gently. Place mixture into tortillas and roll up. Tuck ends under and place in a baking dish. Cover with enchilada sauce, top with cheese and bake about 15 minutes or until heated through.

Serves 6.

ORIENTAL DISHES

Oriental dishes are another quick and easy way to prepare beef. The beef used in these dishes is usually round steak sliced into thin strips. If the meat is slightly frozen it is easier to slice. Slightly frozen beef can also be sliced in a food processor with a wide blade.

Don't worry about making all your vegetable and meat slices perfect for fast and easy cooking. Perfectly cut slices are for food that is going to be photographed for food magazines. It has no place in the life of a busy cook. Just try to make your pieces somewhat the same size so they cook evenly. Here you can use the food processor to really save time.

Stir frying, the method used in the following dishes, means to cook quickly, stirring constantly, with a small amount of oil over a fairly high heat. The wok is the traditional cooking utensil to use for this, but a large skillet will work just as well.

Beef with Cashews

¾ cup water
2 tsp. instant chicken bouillon granules
2 tsp. cornstarch
1 tsp. Chinese 5 Spice
2 T. oil
½ lb. round steak, cut into slices about 2 inches long and ½ inch wide
2 pkgs. frozen Chinese pea pods, thawed by running warm water over them.
⅔ cup unsalted, unroasted cashews

In the water combine the chicken bouillon granules, cornstarch and Chinese 5 Spice. Set aside. In a skillet or wok, place the oil and heat over medium high heat. Add the round steak and stir-fry for about 5 minutes. Add the pea pods and the cashews. Stir for a minute or two. Add the water mixture and stir until thickened. Serve immediately with brown rice or ramen noodles.

Serves 4.

Pepper Beef with Noodles

Ramen noodles are a great, quick side dish for oriental food when you don't have time to cook brown rice. You can find the whole wheat variety in the natural food section of most major grocery stores or at natural food stores.

2 packages, whole wheat ramen noodles
3 T. oil
½ lb. round steak, cut into thin slices, about 2 inches long and ½ inch wide
1 green pepper, cut into thin slices, same size as the beef
6 green onions, cut into 1 inch pieces
2 cloves garlic, minced
optional: 1 piece fresh ginger, about 1 inch long, chopped fine
¼ cup soy sauce
2 tsp. instant beef bouillon granules
2 tsp. cornstarch
¾ cup water

Prepare the ramen according to package directions, but set aside the seasoning packet. In the water stir together the soy sauce, bouillon granules, cornstarch and the seasoning packets left over from the ramen. Set this aside. Place the oil in a wok or skillet over medium high heat. When oil is hot add the beef and stir-fry about five minutes. Add the green pepper, green onion, and if desired fresh ginger. Stir-fry a couple of minutes. Then add the mixture in the water and stir until it thickens. Place stir-fried mixture over drained noodles and serve immediately.

Serves 4.

Hot Oriental Beef Salad

A wonderful luncheon dish for people who like oriental food, but who are tired of the same old thing.

¼ cup soy sauce
2 tsp. honey
1 tsp. Chinese 5 Spice
 dash garlic powder
3 T. oil
1 lb. round steak cut into strips about 2 inches long and about ½ inch wide
1 cup fresh mushrooms, sliced
1 4 oz. can water chestnuts, drained and sliced
1 bunch green onions, chopped
2 tomatoes, cut in chunks
½ cup peanuts, coarsely chopped
3 cups lettuce, shredded

In a cup stir together the soy sauce, honey, and Chinese 5 Spice. Stir until honey is dissolved. Place the oil in a large skillet or wok and heat over medium high heat. Add the round steak and stir-fry about five minutes. Then add the fresh mushrooms, water chestnuts and green onions. Stir-fry a couple more minutes. Finally, add the soy mixture and the tomatoes. Stir-fry gently until heated through. Serve on shredded lettuce and top with chopped peanuts.

Serves 6.

Beef and Green Vegetables

1 6 oz. can
   pineapple juice
¼ cup soy sauce
2 tsp. Chinese 5
   Spice
2 tsp. cornstarch
3 T. oil
½ lb. round steak,
   cut into slices 2
   inches long and
   ½ inch wide
3 sticks of celery,
   sliced
1 green pepper,
   sliced
2 zucchini, sliced
1 pkg. fresh bean
   sprouts
3 green onions,
   sliced

Stir together the pineapple juice, soy sauce, Chinese 5 Spice and the cornstarch. Set aside. In a large skillet or wok place the oil and heat over medium high heat. When oil is hot, add the beef and stir-fry about 5 minutes. Then add the vegetables and stir-fry a few more minutes. Add the liquid mixture and stir until it thickens. Serve over brown rice or ramen.

Serves 6.

BREADS

If some people had to eat their words,
they'd die of indigestion.

BREADS

Homemade breads add something special to any meal and the aroma of bread baking is one of which memories are made.

Breads do not have to be time consuming, yeast breads in order to be all of these special things. Quick rising breads using soda and baking powder as their leavening agents taste great and smell just as yummy as yeast breads while they are cooking.

The major adjustment to bake these breads in under an hour is the size of the bread made. You simply cannot bake large loaves of bread in a regular 5 x 9 inch baking pan and have them ready in one hour. The solution is simple—just bake your breads in smaller pans or in something like an iron skillet that is not very deep and cut the bread into wedges to serve. Another solution is to make muffins that are easy to make and bake in under an hour.

Using the recipes in the following section you'll never again be able to say that you "didn't have enough time" to make bread.

Cheddar Soda Bread

This bread is a variation on the classic Irish Soda Bread. Irish Soda bread looks and tastes like a yeast bread loaf, but it is much easier and quicker to make. This bread and the following two variations add the additional good flavors of cheese and spices to this all time favorite.

1½ **cups whole wheat flour**
½ **cup cornmeal**
1½ **tsp. salt**
1 **tsp. baking soda**
½ **cup grated cheddar cheese**
1 **egg**
2 **T. honey**
1 **cup buttermilk**

Preheat oven to 375°. In a medium size bowl stir together the whole wheat flour, cornmeal, salt and baking soda. Add the grated cheese and stir to coat cheese with flour. In another bowl stir together until well blended the egg, honey and buttermilk. Add the liquid mixture to the flour mixture. Stir to combine the two mixtures.

Turn out of bowl onto a lightly floured surface. If the dough is too sticky, add additional flour. Knead for about 5 minutes. Shape into a round loaf and cut an "x" on top. Place in oven and bake 30-40 minutes or until lightly browned.

Makes 1 round loaf.

Onion Cheddar Bread

Follow recipe as above, but add ¼ cup chopped onions to the dry mixture when you add the cheddar cheese. For an additional variation, use both the tops and the white part of a chopped green onion.

Chili Cheddar Soda Bread

Follow the recipe above, but add ¼ cup of canned, chopped green chilis to the dry mixture when you add the cheddar cheese.

Hint: make this recipe when you have part of a little can of green chilis left over from another recipe.

Cheddar Spice Loaf

2 **cups whole wheat flour**
1½ **tsp. baking powder**
½ **tsp. baking soda**
½ **tsp. salt**
½ **tsp. garlic powder**
½ **tsp. marjoram**
1 **cup shredded or chopped cheddar cheese**
1 **cup buttermilk**
¼ **cup safflower or corn oil**
2 **eggs**

In a large bowl stir together the whole wheat flour, baking powder, baking soda, salt, garlic powder, and marjoram. Add the cheddar cheese and stir to coat the cheese with flour mixture. In another bowl stir until well blended the buttermilk, oil, and eggs. Add this to the flour mixture and stir until just blended. Spoon into two well greased 3½ x 7 bread pans and bake at 375° about 30-45 minutes or until a pick inserted in the center comes out clean.

Makes 2 small loaves.

Pineapple Walnut Bread

This is a nice, mild bread for breakfast. It goes especially well with a bowl of mixed fruit and a glass of milk.

2 T. oil
½ cup honey
2 beaten eggs
1 cup crushed pineapple and juice
¼ cup milk
2 cups whole wheat flour
2 tsp. baking powder
½ tsp. salt
¾ cup walnuts, chopped

In a medium sized bowl combine the butter, honey, eggs, pineapple, milk and vanilla. In another bowl stir together the flour, baking powder, salt and walnuts. Combine the two mixtures, using just a few strokes. Pour into two 3½ x 7 loaf pans and bake at 350° for 45 minutes or until a toothpick inserted in the center comes out clean.

Makes 2 small loaves.

Applesauce Bran Bread

Another nice bread for breakfast or mid-morning snack. This bread is baked in an iron skillet and cut into wedges to serve.

2½ cups whole wheat flour
½ cup bran
1½ tsp. baking powder
½ tsp. baking soda
½ tsp. salt
½ tsp. cinnamon
¼ cup oil
2 eggs
½ cup honey
1¼ cups milk
1 tsp. vanilla
1 cup applesauce

Preheat oven to 375°. Grease well a 10 inch iron skillet. In one bowl stir together the whole wheat flour, bran, baking powder, soda, salt and cinnamon. In another bowl combine the oil, eggs, honey, milk, cinnamon, vanilla and applesauce. Stir the two mixtures together, using as few strokes as possible. Pour into greased pan and bake about 30 minutes or until a toothpick inserted in the center comes out clean. Allow to cool about 10 minutes and cut into wedges to serve.

Makes 1 round loaf.

Sunflower Skillet Bread

Also cooked in a skillet, this bread is nice served with soup.

2¼ cups whole wheat
    flour
1 cup raw sunflower
    seeds
1½ tsp. baking
    powder
½ tsp. baking soda
½ tsp. salt
⅓ cup oil
2 eggs
½ cup honey
1½ cups milk
1 tsp. vanilla
2 T. sunflower seeds

Preheat oven to 375°. Grease well a 10 inch iron skillet. In one bowl stir together the whole wheat flour, baking powder, soda, salt and sunflower seeds. In another combine the oil, eggs, honey, milk and vanilla. Combine the two mixtures, stirring as little as possible. Pour into skillet and sprinkle sunflower seeds on top. Bake for about 30 minutes or until a toothpick inserted in the center comes out clean. Allow to cool about 10 minutes and cut into wedges to serve.

Makes 1 round loaf.

Herb Onion Skillet Bread

2½ cups whole wheat
    flour
1½ tsp. baking
    powder
½ tsp. soda
½ tsp. salt
½ tsp. garlic powder
1 tsp. basil
¼ tsp. oregano
¼ tsp. thyme
¼ cup oil
2 eggs
½ cup honey
1½ cups milk
1 onion, finely
    chopped

Preheat oven to 375°. Grease well a 10 inch iron skillet. In one bowl combine the whole wheat flour, baking powder, soda, salt, garlic powder, basil, oregano and thyme. In another combine the oil, eggs, honey, milk and onion. Stir the two mixtures together using as few strokes as possible. Pour into skillet and bake about 30 minutes or until a toothpick inserted in the center comes out clean. Allow to cool about 10 minutes, cut into wedges and serve.

Makes 1 round loaf.

Skillet Yogurt Cornbread

It has always been my favorite way to make cornbread by baking it in an iron skillet. If you want the crust extra crispy, add 3 tablespoons of oil to the greased pan and heat it in the oven for about 10 minutes before you pour the batter in.

1¼ cups whole wheat flour
1¼ cups cornmeal
1 tsp. baking powder
1 tsp. baking soda
1 cup plain yogurt
⅓ cup honey
2 eggs
¼ cup milk
¼ cup melted butter or margarine

Preheat oven to 400°. Grease well a 10 inch iron skillet. In one bowl combine the whole wheat flour, cornmeal, baking powder, and baking soda. In another combine well the yogurt, honey, eggs, milk and melted butter or margarine. Stir together the two mixtures using as few strokes as possible. Pour into skillet and bake for about 30 minutes or until golden brown. Cut into wedges to serve.

Makes 1 round loaf.

Apple Muffins

These are great for breakfast, but they are also a nice afternoon snack as well.

1¾ cups whole wheat flour
½ cup walnuts
1 T. baking powder
½ tsp. nutmeg
½ tsp. salt
2 eggs
¼ cup oil
1 cup milk
¼ cup honey
1 cup shredded apple

Preheat oven to 400°. Grease well one dozen muffin cups. In one bowl combine the flour, walnuts, baking powder, nutmeg, and salt. In another combine well the eggs, oil, milk, honey and shredded apple. Stir the two mixtures together using as few strokes as possible. Spoon into muffin cups and bake about 20 minutes or until lightly browned.

Makes 12.

Pear Walnut Muffins

Follow the recipe above, but substitute one cup of chopped, ripe pear for the cup of shredded apple.

Cheese Muffins

The cheesy flavor in these is wonderful.

1¾ cups whole wheat
    flour
1 T. baking powder
½ tsp. salt
¾ cup cheddar
    cheese, grated
2 eggs
¼ cup oil
1 cup milk
¼ cup honey
    Parmesan cheese

Preheat oven to 400°. Grease well 12 muffin cups. In one bowl stir together the whole wheat flour, baking powder, and salt. Add cheddar cheese and stir together. In another bowl combine well the eggs, oil, milk and honey. Stir mixtures together using as few strokes as possible. Spoon into muffin cups. Sprinkle the Parmesan cheese on top. Bake about 20 minutes or until lightly browned.
    Makes 12 muffins.

Cornmeal Muffins

1 cup whole wheat
    flour
¾ cup cornmeal
1 T. baking powder
½ tsp. salt
⅓ cup frozen corn,
    thawed
2 eggs
¼ cup oil
1 cup milk
¼ cup honey

Preheat oven to 400°. Grease well 12 muffin cups. In one bowl combine the whole wheat flour, cornmeal, baking powder, and salt. Stir in corn. In another bowl combine the eggs, oil, milk and honey. Combine the two mixtures using as few strokes as possible. Spoon into muffin cups and bake for about 20-30 minutes or until golden brown.
    Makes 12 muffins.

BREAKFAST
AND
BRUNCH
IDEAS

A smile is the light in the window of your face
to let others know your heart is at home.

BREAKFAST AND BRUNCH IDEAS

Not only for breakfast and brunch, but for any time of day the recipes in this section are quick and delicious. Pancake suppers are great fun and granolas and other hot cereals make a satisfying light dinner.

For good health, nutritionists tell us that breakfast is the most important meal of the day. It's important for other reasons also. It replenishes our body after its night long fast. It gives our bodies and brains the fuel needed to think and work. It is also a time to communicate with the people we love, to touch them before the day fragments our lives.

So take the time to get up a little earlier to make breakfast for the ones you love, to see each other and to share together before the busy day begins.

PANCAKES

There are endless delicious variations in the making of pancakes: blueberry, banana walnut, corn, honey-nut and many more. Whatever variety you choose, the following hints will help make your pancakes perfect.

Pancake hints
—For fluffy, light pancakes, just barely stir the dry and wet ingredients together. Don't worry about lumps. Too much stirring will toughen the batter.
—Use your heaviest, well seasoned skillet or griddle to cook pancakes on. Grease lightly with vegetable oil. Just brush it on and repeat between batches of pancakes. The griddle is hot enough when a drop of water dances on it a few minutes before evaporating. If it evaporates right away the griddle is too hot.
—Always make a test pancake first, both to test the temperature of the griddle and to test the thickness of the batter. Because various flours vary in their moisture content, you may want to either add a little milk or water to thin the batter or a little bit of flour to thicken it. You almost always have to adjust the liquid and flour balance not only because of the moisture content of the various ingredients, but according to your personal preference for either thin or thick pancakes.
—A pancake is done on one side when the bubbles forming around the edges are starting to break and bubbles are just starting to form in the center. Turn pancakes only once. The second side takes about half as long as the first to cook.
—If not served right away, pancakes can be kept warm in a 200° oven. If at all possible, keep them separated by tea towels. If they are stacked on one another for very long, they can get soggy.

Note on Pancake Toppings
Don't just stop with maple syrup and butter as a topping for pancakes, though it is hard to beat. Just be sure you use real maple syrup and not the maple flavored sugar syrups that fill the market shelves. It does cost more, but it is definitely worth it.
In addition to maple syrup, there are as many varieties of toppings for pancakes as there are kinds of pancakes. The recipes for these start on page 65.

Whole Wheat Buttermilk Pancakes

Simple and delicious. Easy to make any time if you use the powdered buttermilk.

1¼ cups whole wheat
    flour
1 tsp. baking
    powder
½ tsp. baking soda
½ tsp. salt
1¼ cups buttermilk
1 egg
2 T. vegetable oil
2 T. honey (heated
    till runny)

In a medium size bowl stir together the dry ingredients. In another bowl stir together the buttermilk, egg, vegetable oil and honey. Combine the two mixtures, using as few strokes as possible. Adjust the thickness of the batter, adding either flour or liquid. Cook on a heated griddle.

Makes about 12 4 inch cakes.

Honey Nut Pancakes

You can substitute any nut for the pecans in this recipe, or a combination of nuts can be used.

1½ cups whole wheat
    flour
⅔ cup chopped
    pecans
½ tsp. salt
1½ tsp. baking
    powder
2 eggs
3 T. honey (heated
    till runny)
3 T. butter or
    margarine, melted
1¼ cups milk

In a large bowl stir together the flour, pecans, salt and baking powder. In another bowl mix well the eggs, honey, butter or margarine and milk. Combine the two mixtures, using as few strokes as possible. Adjust the thickness of the batter by adding either flour or liquid as desired. Bake on a hot griddle or skillet.

Makes about 14 4 inch cakes.

Banana Walnut Pancakes

These are one of my favorites, absolutely delicious. Fairly ripe bananas taste the best in the pancakes.

1¼ cups whole wheat flour
1 tsp. salt
1½ tsp. baking powder
¼ cup chopped walnuts
2 eggs
3 T. honey (heated till runny)
3 T. oil
1-1¼ cups milk
2 bananas, sliced

In a large bowl combine the flour, salt, baking powder and walnuts. In another bowl mix thoroughly the eggs, honey, oil and milk. Stir together the two mixtures using as few strokes as possible. Adjust the thickness of the batter by adding either flour or liquid as desired. Cook on a heated griddle or skillet by dropping on several spoonsful of batter and then placing several banana slices on each pancake. Cook on that side, turn over and finish cooking.

Makes about 14 4 inch pancakes.

Blueberry Pancakes

Fresh blueberries, of course, are wonderful, but frozen blueberries work quite nicely also. Just thaw them first by running hot water over them and allow them to drain a few minutes before using.

1¼ cups whole wheat flour
½ tsp. salt
1½ tsp. baking powder
1 cup blueberries, fresh or frozen and thawed
2 eggs
3 T. honey (heated till runny)
3 T. oil
1¼ cups milk

In a large bowl combine the whole wheat flour, salt and baking powder. Gently stir the blueberries into the flour mixture. In another bowl combine well the eggs, honey, oil and milk. Add liquid to dry mixture, using as few strokes as possible. Adjust the thickness of the batter by adding either flour or liquid as desired. Bake on a heated griddle or skillet.

Makes about 15 4 inch pancakes.

Cottage Cheese Pancakes

These moist pancakes are very high in protein because of the added cottage cheese. They are especially good served with applesauce on top or the Sauteed Apple Slices page 67.

1¼ cups whole wheat
     flour
  1 tsp. salt
  2 tsp. baking
     powder
     dash nutmeg
  ¾ cup cottage
     cheese
  1 egg
  3 T. honey (heated
     till runny)
  3 T. oil
  1 cup milk
  ¼ cup plain yogurt

In a large bowl stir together the whole wheat flour, salt, baking powder and nutmeg. Gently stir in the cottage cheese. In another bowl combine well the egg, honey, oil, milk and yogurt. Stir together the two mixtures with as few strokes as possible. Bake on a heated griddle or skillet.

Makes about 16 4 inch pancakes.

 ## Crispy Corn Pancakes

Corn pancakes used to be called "johnny cakes." Whatever you call them they are yummy. Plain maple syrup and lots of real butter taste best on these.

  ¾ cup whole wheat
     flour
  ¾ cup corn meal
  1 tsp. salt
  2 tsp. baking
     powder
  ¾ cup frozen corn,
     thawed
  1 egg
  3 T. honey (heated
     till runny)
  3 T. melted butter or
     margarine
1¼ cups milk

In a large bowl stir together the flour, corn meal, salt and baking powder. Gently stir in the corn. In another bowl combine the eggs, honey, melted butter or margarine and milk. Combine the two mixtures using as few strokes as possible. Adjust the thickness of the batter by adding either flour or liquid as desired. Bake on a heated griddle or skillet.

Makes about 16 4 inch pancakes.

Whole Wheat Baked German Pancake

2 T. butter or
   margarine,
   softened
3 eggs
⅔ cup whole wheat
   flour
⅔ cup milk
½ tsp. salt
2 T. butter, melted

This big, yummy pancake can either be served as a breakfast main dish for two to four people or a dessert for six to eight. It is always served with a topping, either the traditional powdered sugar and freshly squeezed lemon, a butter almond topping or a tangy apple topping. The recipe for Sauteed Apple Slices, my personal favorite topping for this pancake, is on page 68 .

Preheat oven to 450°. Grease a 10 inch heavy skillet with the margarine or butter. Place all ingredients in a large bowl and beat until well blended. Pour batter into skillet and place in oven. Bake for 20 minutes. Remove, place on serving platter and cover with desired topping, page 67.
Serves 3-8.

BREAKFAST SANDWICHES

If you're in a hurry and need something to eat while commuting to work or school, or if you would just like something different for breakfast, try some of the breakfast sandwiches below. They are quick, healthy and delicious.

Fried Egg Sandwich

For some reason, I like my egg really crispy in this sandwich, but your personal preference determines how you cook your egg. You could also scramble a couple of eggs if you desire.

Fried Egg Sandwich, continued

1 tsp. butter or
margarine
1 egg
2 slices whole
wheat bread
alfalfa sprouts
mayonnaise
optional: 1 slice
cheddar cheese

In a small skillet melt the butter or margarine. Break one egg into the skillet and break up the yolk. Cook until solid. Toast the bread while egg is cooking. Spread the bread with the mayonnaise and sprouts and, if desired, top with the cheese. Add egg.
Serves 1.

Eggs and Cheese in Pita

2 eggs, scrambled
¼ cup shredded
cheese, jack or
cheddar is good
mayonnaise
dash salt and
pepper
alfalfa sprouts
1 piece whole wheat
pita bread

Combine scrambled eggs, cheese, mayonnaise to moisten, and dash of salt and pepper. Place in halves of pita bread with sprouts.
Serves 1.

Scrambled Eggs and Mushrooms in Pita

2 tsp. butter or
margarine
¼ cup fresh
mushrooms, sliced
2 green onions,
chopped
2 eggs
mayonnaise
alfalfa sprouts
whole wheat pita
bread

In a small skillet melt the butter or margarine. Add the mushrooms and onions and saute until the mushrooms are soft. Add eggs and scramble. Put a thin layer of mayonnaise in the pita bread, add sprouts and the egg and mushroom mixture.
Serves 1.

Mushroom Asparagus Strata

In many traditional recipes for stratas, the instructions state that the strata should be prepared the night before and left in the refrigerator overnight before it is cooked. That method definitely would not fit into this present cookbook under the guidelines that foods be prepared in under an hour. With much fear that some strange thing would happen, I created this quick version. It is delicious and so easy. Try it for a light lunch or supper as well as breakfast.

1   9 oz. package frozen asparagus, thawed by running hot water over it

1   cup fresh mushrooms, cut up

4   slices whole wheat bread, torn into little pieces

3   green onions, sliced

2   T. soft butter or margarine

5   eggs

2   cups jack cheese, shredded

1¾   cups milk dash salt and pepper

In a large bowl toss together the asparagus, fresh mushrooms, bread pieces and green onions. Grease a 9 x 13 baking pan with the soft butter or margarine. Place the vegetable and bread mixture into this pan. In another bowl stir together the eggs, cheese, milk and salt and pepper. Pour this over the mixture in the pan. Set aside for 15 minutes. Bake in a 350° oven for 30 minutes.

Serves 6.

Variations: You can substitute approximately 2 cups of any other variety of fresh or frozen vegetables for the asparagus and the mushrooms. Broccoli, summer squash, and tomatoes are just a few of the possibilities. Any combination of vegetables that would work in a quiche will also work in a strata.

Breakfast Mini Pizzas

Yummy little treats. You can make one just for yourself or make a whole batch for a teenagers' brunch.

2 English muffin
   halves
2 tsp. butter or
   margarine
¼ cup fresh
   mushrooms,
   chopped
1 green onion,
   chopped
1 egg
1 T. black olives,
   sliced
   catsup
   oregano
¼ cup grated
   mozzarella cheese

Briefly toast English muffin halves. In a small skillet melt the butter or margarine. Saute the mushrooms and onions until the mushrooms are soft. Add the egg and scramble it. Add the black olives. Place a little catsup on top of toasted English muffin, sprinkle on a dash of oregano. Top with egg mixture. Place mozzarella cheese on top. Heat briefly in oven or microwave until cheese melts.

Serves 1.

Breakfast Burritos

Similar to the breakfast sandwiches, you use a flour tortilla instead of pita or regular bread.

1 whole wheat flour
   tortilla
1 egg, scrambled
1 slice cheese, cut
   into little pieces,
   jack or cheddar is
   nice
2 slices avocado,
   cut into chunks
   taco sauce or
   salsa

Place the flour tortilla on the counter, add the egg, cheese and avocado. Drizzle on taco sauce or salsa. Roll up tortilla and tuck in ends. Ready to eat as is or it can be heated briefly in oven or microwave.

Serves 1.

WHOLE WHEAT FRENCH TOAST

After you've tried French toast with whole wheat bread, you'll wonder how you ever enjoyed the bland variety made with white bread. Not only is the taste so much better, but eating a few slices of whole wheat French toast in the mornings gives you a good start on your body's need for fiber during the day.

Homemade whole wheat bread or the really heavy, grainy purchased varieties make the best French toast.

 ## Basic Whole Wheat French Toast

Select any of the toppings on page 65 for a wonderful breakfast treat.

2 **eggs, beaten**	In a shallow, flat bottomed bowl combine the eggs, milk, vanilla, nutmeg and salt. Dip the slices of whole wheat bread in this mixture and then fry on a well buttered skillet or griddle until browned on each side.
¾ **cup milk**	
½ **tsp. vanilla**	
¼ **tsp. nutmeg**	
dash salt	
8 **slices whole**	**Note:** For added nutrition and texture, after dipping the bread in the egg and milk mixture, dip it into plain wheat germ before frying it.
wheat bread	Serves 2-4.

Tropical French Toast

2 **eggs, beaten**
¼ **cup milk**
½ **cup pineapple juice**
½ **cup wheat germ**
½ **cup finely grated coconut**
8 **slices whole wheat bread**

This is an especially delicious French toast. It is very nice to serve for a special brunch. Try the Sauteed Banana Slices (page 68) on top for a special treat.

In a shallow, flat bottomed bowl combine the eggs, milk and pineapple juice. Combine the wheat germ and coconut on a plate. Dip the bread first into the liquid mixture and then into the wheat germ and coconut mixture. Fry on a well buttered griddle or skillet until golden brown.

Serves 2-4.

GRANOLAS AND OTHER CEREALS

Mention granola and a whole world of natural and healthful foods come to mind. And they should. Granola with its mixture of whole grains, nuts and dried fruits really is a wonderful food, high in fiber and numerous vitamins and minerals. Granola is especially good for you if you make your own, a process that takes only minutes to do.

In addition to eating granola for cold cereal, try some whole grains with nuts and dried fruits for hot cereal. These are quite satisfying and yummy. Don't reserve hot cereals for breakfast time only. They make a good light dinner, especially on cold evenings.

In the following recipes the amounts can be varied to suit your individual taste. If you prefer more nuts or fruits, go ahead and add them. The cereals can be made without any salt and you can cut down on the amount of sweetner used if you wish to cut down on calories.

Coconut Walnut Granola

Regular raisins can be used in place of the golden raisins, but the golden ones add a special touch.

4 cups oat flakes
1 cup unsweetened coconut
1 cup chopped walnuts
½ cup wheat germ
½ cup safflower oil
½ cup honey
1 tsp. vanilla
1 cup golden raisins

Preheat oven to 325°. In a large bowl stir together the oat flakes, coconut, walnuts and wheat germ. In a small pan heat together the safflower oil, vanilla and honey. Pour over the granola mixture and toss to coat well. Place on two cookie sheets and toast in oven until lightly golden brown, about 15-20 minutes. Stir a couple of times in the baking process and be careful not to overcook. Remove from oven, cool and stir in raisins.

Makes about 7 cups.

Apple Granola

4 cups oat flakes
½ cup wheat germ
½ cup sunflower seeds, raw and unsalted
½ cup raw cashews, in pieces
½ tsp. salt
½ cup safflower oil
½ cup honey
1 cup dried apple pieces

Preheat oven to 325°. In a large bowl stir together the oat flakes, wheat germ, sunflower seeds, cashews and salt. In a small pan heat together the safflower oil and honey. Pour over the grain mixture and stir to coat well. Place on two cookie sheets and bake, stirring a couple of times until golden brown. Do not overcook. Remove from oven, cool and stir in dried apple pieces.

Makes about 6½ cups.

Almond Granola

The especially delicious aroma you will smell while this is baking comes from the almond extract.

4 cups rolled oats
1 cup wheat germ
2 cups sliced almonds
1 tsp. salt
½ cup safflower oil
½ cup honey
1 tsp. almond extract

Preheat oven to 325°. In a large bowl stir together the oat flakes, wheat germ, and sliced almonds. In a small pan heat together, until honey melts, the safflower oil, honey and almond extract. Pour over the grain mixture and stir to coat well. Place on two cookie sheets in the oven and bake until golden brown, stirring a few times during baking. Do not overcook. Remove from oven and cool. Makes about 7 cups.

 # Cracked Wheat Hot Cereal

This is my personal, all time favorite hot cereal. It has a delicious, hearty, whole wheat taste, a crunchy texture and is very easy and quick to make.

1 cup cracked wheat
2 cups water
dash salt

In a medium size sauce pan bring the water to a boil, add salt and stir in cracked wheat. Cover, turn down heat and allow to simmer for about 15 minutes. It's now ready to eat with your favorite topping. Most delicious to me is warm milk, a pat of butter and a little real maple syrup. Serves 2-4.

Cinnamon Honey Oatmeal

After this spicy treat, you'll never be satisfied with plain oatmeal again.

3 cups water
1 cup oatmeal
¼ tsp. salt
¼ tsp. cinnamon
3 T. walnuts, chopped
2 T. raisins
2 T. honey

In a medium size saucepan, bring water to a boil. In another bowl, stir together the oatmeal, salt, cinnamon, walnuts and raisins. Add to boiling water, cover and cook until oatmeal is done, from 10 to 20 minutes depending on the kind of oatmeal. Just before taking off stove, stir in honey. Serve with milk. Serves 4.

Apple Oatmeal

This version is based on the European muesli cereals, the popular combinations of apples, nuts and grains for breakfast.

3 cups water
1 cup oatmeal
¼ tsp. salt
¼ cup sliced almonds
¼ cup dried apples, chopped

In a medium saucepan heat the water to boiling. Add oatmeal, salt, almonds and apples. Turn down heat and cook until oatmeal is done, from 10 to 20 minutes depending upon the type of oatmeal purchased. Serve with milk and honey. Serves 4.

FRUIT FOR BREAKFAST

Long ago the English found that an orange a day prevented scurvy, the dread disease that took the lives of many sailors on long voyages. Vitamin C is the almost magical ingredient in oranges that is essential for health. Though we no longer worry about scurvy on long voyages, our need for vitamin C has not changed. It is still an essential dietary requirement for good health.

Fruit, especially citrus fruit, is one of the best sources of vitamin C. Fruits contain numerous other vitamins and minerals and are a valuable dietary source of fiber. Breakfast is a wonderful time to eat fruit, setting your day off to a healthy start. Fruits also complement the sometimes heavier meal items at breakfast such as breads and grains.

Oranges and Yogurt

3 oranges
1 T. honey
½ cup vanilla yogurt
½ tsp. cinnamon

Peel and slice oranges crosswise in thin layers. Arrange on a platter. Spoon vanilla yogurt in center and drizzle honey over it. Sprinkle on cinnamon.
Serves 4.

Watermelon Treat

The color combination of this dish is fantastic.

4 wedges of watermelon
1 cup fresh blueberries
juice of one half fresh lime

Place watermelon wedges on serving plates. In a small bowl toss together the blueberries and the fresh lime juice. Spoon blueberries over watermelon wedges and serve.
Serves 4.

Cantaloupe Hawaiian

This also makes a nice luncheon salad. Coconut flakes can also be added for variety or garnish.

4 wedges of
cantaloupe
1 cup fresh
pineapple pieces
½ cup fresh
strawberries
¼ cup orange juice

Place cantaloupe on serving plates. In a small bowl combine the pineapple, strawberries and orange juice. Spoon over cantaloupe and serve.
Serves 4.

Granola Topped Baked Apples

Served hot or cold, these are delicious for breakfast or brunch. They are also a nice fruit dessert.

2 apples
¼ cup granola
¼ cup walnuts,
chopped
¼ tsp. cinnamon
¼ tsp. nutmeg
2 T. honey
2 T. butter or
margarine
½ cup water or apple
juice

Cut apples in half and cut out the core. Slice a small piece off the bottom so apples will sit flat. Place in a baking dish. Cut the pieces of apple slices into little chunks. Combine apple chunks with granola, walnuts, cinnamon and nutmeg. In a small pan heat butter and honey until melted. Stir together with the granola apple mixture. Mound on top of apple halves. Pour water or apple juice into pan. Cover and bake in 350° oven for 30 minutes. Remove cover, baste and bake about 10 more minutes. Serve with milk or light cream.
Serves 4.

Honey Baked Grapefruit

2 grapefruit
½ cup shredded
    coconut
¼ cup honey

Cut grapefruit in half and cut through sections for serving. Top each half with coconut and then drizzle on honey. Pre-heat broiler in oven and broil for about 5 minutes. Serve immediately.

Serves 4.

BREAKFAST TOPPINGS

When you tire of maple syrup or want something special for your homemade pancakes and French toast, try some of the delicious toppings below. They taste so good and are much less expensive to make than some of the fancy gourmet toppings and syrups sold in specialty food shops. In addition, all the flavors and ingredients are natural.

Besides being wonderful breakfast toppings, most of these make delicious ice cream toppings as well.

Blueberry Syrup

½ cup honey
½ cup blueberries,
    fresh or frozen
¼ tsp. coriander
¼ tsp. grated lemon
    rind

In a medium saucepan over medium heat, gently heat together the honey and blueberries. Add coriander and lemon rind, stir and serve.

Makes about 1 cup.

Cranberry Syrup

Follow the recipe for Blueberry Syrup, but substitute fresh or frozen cranberries for the blueberries.

Maple Butter Honey

1 **cup honey**
3 **T. butter**
½ **tsp. maple extract**

In a small saucepan heat honey and butter together over medium heat until butter melts. Stir in maple extract.
Makes about 1 cup.

Almond Honey

¾ **cup honey**
¼ **tsp. almond extract**
½ **cup sliced almonds**
2 **T. butter**

Heat together in a small saucepan over medium heat the honey, almond extract, almonds and butter until butter melts.
Makes about 1¼ cups.

Whipped Honey Butter

½ **cup butter, softened**
¼ **cup honey**
¼ **cup whipping cream**
½ **tsp. vanilla**

In a small bowl beat butter until fluffy. Add honey and combine well. Stir vanilla into whipping cream and beat in. Keep chilled until serving time.
Makes about 1 cup.

Dark Cherry Syrup

1 16 oz. can
  unsweetened dark
  cherries
2 T. honey
1 tsp. grated lemon
  peel
¼ cup water
4 tsp. cornstarch

In a medium skillet place the cherries, including the juice, honey, and lemon peel. Warm slowly over low heat. Combine the 4 teaspoons of cornstarch with the ¼ cup water and stir into the cherry mixture. Continue to heat, stirring constantly until mixture thickens and clears.

Makes about 2 cups.

Date Nut Butter

1 cup butter,
  softened
2 T. honey
2 T. chopped dates
¼ cup chopped
  walnuts

In a medium bowl beat butter and honey together until fluffy. Gently stir in dates and nuts.

Makes about 1¼ cups.

Sauteed Apple Slices

3 T. butter
2 apples, sliced
2 T. honey
½ tsp. cinnamon
½ tsp. coriander
  optional: ¼ cup
  raisins
  optional: ¼ cup
  chopped walnuts

Melt the butter in a medium skillet over medium heat. Add the apple slices and cook a few minutes. Add the honey, cinnamon, coriander and, if desired, raisins and walnuts. Continue to cook, stirring gently until apples are tender, about 20 minutes.

Makes about 2 cups.

Sauteed Banana Slices

3 T. butter
4 bananas, sliced
2 T. lemon juice
3 T. honey
¼ tsp. nutmeg
    optional: ¼ cup
    chopped walnuts
    or pecans

Melt the butter in a medium skillet over medium heat. Toss the banana slices in lemon. Add the banana slices, honey and nutmeg and, if desired, the nuts, to the skillet. Cook gently until banana pieces are tender.

Makes about 2 cups.

CHICKEN
AND
TURKEY

*Let your food for thought always contain
the element of goodness.*

CHICKEN AND TURKEY

Chicken and turkey can be cooked easily and deliciously in so many ways. Poultry is much lower in fat than beef, making it also lower in cholesterol and calories. It also is usually quite low in cost, making it a plus for any budget.

Chicken and turkey fit quite well into the scheme of fast cooking, particularly if you just cook individual pieces such as chicken thighs, boned chicken breasts, and slices of turkey breast. The last two, the boned chicken breasts and slices of turkey breast are amazingly versatile. You can use them for quick dinners or elegant entrees and they can be cut up to be stir-fried.

You can either cut your own slices of turkey breast, or you can buy packages of the slices already cut. In the same way you can bone your own chicken breasts or buy them already boned. Of course, to do it yourself is cheaper, but you do have more waste if you do it yourself, and it does take longer. If time is of great concern, sometimes it is worth it to have the pieces already cut to order.

Another advantage of the boned chicken breasts and sliced turkey breast is that because they are rather thin slices of meat, they thaw very quickly. This makes them an excellent food to always have on hand for a quick and delicious meal. I like to buy them in the bulk family packages, which are cheaper, and then take them home and refreeze them in individual portions.

Though the recipes are divided into some for turkey and some for chicken, you can really use either meat for any recipe.

Because of their delicious taste, universal appeal, and ease of preparation, the following recipes are some of my most favorite when entertaining.

Turkey Breast Slices with Spring Vegetables

In the spring you can also use fresh vegetables in place of the frozen ones called for in the recipe below.

1 cup frozen peas
1 10 oz. package frozen asparagus pieces
4 turkey breast slices
  whole wheat flour
3 T. butter or margarine
1 T. oil
1 T. whole wheat flour
1 cup chicken broth
½ cup cream or half and half
  salt and pepper

Place frozen peas and asparagus in a colander. Run warm water over them until thawed. Dip turkey breast slices into flour. In a large skillet melt the butter or margarine and add the oil. Saute the turkey slices until golden brown, 3-5 minutes on each side. Remove and keep warm. Add whole wheat flour to pan and stir, scraping bottom well. Cook for a minute or so. Add chicken broth and cook stirring constantly until it begins to thicken. Add cream or half and half and salt and pepper. Cook a minute, then add peas and asparagus. Heat through. Place turkey breast slices on a serving platter and pour this mixture over them. Serve immediately.
Serves 4.

Lemon Pepper Turkey Breast Slices

4 turkey breast slices
¼ cup fresh lemon juice
  lemon pepper
4 slices fresh lemon

Preheat oven to 375°. In a shallow baking dish place the turkey slices. Spoon over them the lemon juice. Sprinkle on the lemon pepper. Top each slice with a slice of lemon. Cover and bake for 20 minutes, or until done.
Serves 4.

Turkey Breast Slices with Mushroom Sauce

One of my favorites for a company dinner.

2　T. butter or
　　margarine
1　cup fresh
　　mushrooms,
　　cleaned and sliced
¼　cup green onions,
　　chopped
4　turkey breast
　　slices
4　T. butter or
　　margarine
1　cup carbonated
　　white grape juice
½　tsp. soy sauce
½　tsp. Worchester-
　　shire sauce
　　salt and pepper to
　　taste

In a small skillet melt the 2 tablespoons butter or margarine. Add the mushrooms and the green onions and cook until mushrooms are tender. Set aside.

Dip turkey breast slices into flour and place in a large skillet. Saute them in the melted butter or margarine until they are golden brown, about 3-5 minutes on each side. After they have been sauteed, set aside, keeping warm. Pour grape juice, soy sauce and Worchestershire sauce into pan. Stir and allow to cook down slightly. Add salt, pepper, reserved mushrooms and green onions. Pour over turkey breasts and serve immediately.

Serves 4.

Creamy Mushroom Turkey Breast Slices

For a richer version of the above recipe, reduce the amount of grape juice to ½ cup and use ½ cup whipping cream. Proceed as above.

Serves 4.

Turkey Breast Slices with Tarragon

Tarragon gives its distinctive flavor to this dish. Dried tarragon works well, but if you are able to use fresh, you are in for an even better taste treat.

4 T. butter or
   margarine
4 turkey breast
   slices
   whole wheat flour
2 T. shallots or
   green onions,
   finely chopped
1 cup carbonated
   white grape juice
1 tsp. dried tarragon
   dash salt and
   pepper

In a large skillet melt the butter or margarine. Dip the turkey breast slices in flour and saute until golden brown, 3-5 minutes on each side. Remove and keep warm. Add shallots or green onions and cook a few minutes. Add white grape juice and tarragon. Cook, stirring constantly for 1 minute. Place turkey breast slices on a serving platter and pour sauce over. Serve immediately.
Serves 4.

 ## Herb Baked Turkey Breast Slices

Light, yet very nutritious, this is a good recipe when dieting. You can cut down the amount of butter used if desired and you can also substitute diet margarine for the butter.

4 turkey breast
   slices
⅓ cup butter,
   softened
2 tsp. fresh lemon
   juice
2 T. chopped
   parsley
¼ tsp. dried thyme
1 green onion, very
   finely chopped

Preheat oven to 375°. Place turkey breast slices in a baking dish. In a small bowl place the butter, lemon juice, parsley, thyme and green onion. Stir together to combine. Spread mixture over each turkey breast slice. Bake for about 20 minutes or until done, basting once or twice.
Serves 4.

Turkey Breast Slices Veronique

This is a variation of a classic French dish made the easy, healthful way while retaining the classic, delicate flavor.

3 **T. butter or margarine**
4 **turkey breast slices**
1 **cup white carbonated grape juice**
1 **cup seedless green grapes**

Melt butter in a large skillet. Cut turkey slices into 4 strips each. Saute in butter until golden, about 6 minutes. Pour carbonated grape juice over and add green grapes. Cover and simmer 10 minutes and serve.

Serves 4.

 # Turkey Breast Slices Dijon

Be sure to use a good Dijon mustard in this recipe, and don't be tempted under any circumstances to substitute the old hot dog variety.

3 **T. butter or margarine**
4 **turkey breast slices**
  whole wheat flour
½ **cup chicken broth**
½ **cup half and half**
2 **T. Dijon style mustard**
  salt and pepper

In a large skillet melt the butter or margarine. Dip the turkey breast slices in flour and saute until golden brown, 3-5 minutes on each side. Remove from skillet and set aside. Pour chicken broth into skillet and stir a minute, add half and half, mustard, and salt and pepper. Stir to combine and heat through. Place turkey slices on a serving platter, pour sauce over and serve.

Serves 4.

Chicken Tosca

This is an Italian-type flavored dish. It is great served either over or alongside pasta.

3 T. olive or
   vegetable oil
4 boned chicken
   breasts
   flour
1 8 oz. can tomato
   sauce
   dash salt and
   pepper
¼ tsp. basil
   dash garlic
   powder
   dash oregano
4 slices provolone
   or mozzarella
   cheese

Pound the chicken breasts to flatten them slightly. In a large skillet heat the oil. Dip the chicken breasts in flour and saute until golden brown, 3-5 minutes on each side. Mix together the tomato sauce, garlic powder, oregano, salt, pepper and basil. Pour over chicken. Top each slice with cheese. Cover and simmer for 10 minutes and serve.
Serves 4.

Chicken Breasts Piccata

The taste of this dish is very similar to Weiner snitzel made with veal, and it is fantastic.

3 T. butter
4 boned chicken
   breasts
   flour
   juice of one lemon
½ cup carbonated
   white grape juice
   dash salt and
   pepper
4 thin slices lemon

Pound chicken breasts slightly to flatten. In a large skillet melt the butter. Dip the chicken breasts in flour and saute until golden brown in the butter, about 3-5 minutes on each side. Just before done, spoon lemon juice over each. Remove from skillet and keep warm. Pour grape juice into pan and stir, add salt and pepper, cook 2 minutes. Pour over cooked breasts, top each with a lemon slice and serve.
Serves 4.

Chicken with Artichokes

This makes a very nice company dinner as well as a special one just for the family.

2 T. butter
1 6½ oz. jar
  artichoke hearts
4 boned chicken
  breasts
  flour
½ cup fresh
  mushrooms, sliced
½ cup chicken broth
½ cup lemon juice
  dash salt and
  pepper

Pound chicken breasts slightly to flatten. In a large skillet melt the butter. Drain the liquid from the artichoke hearts and add this to the skillet. Dip the chicken breasts in flour and saute until golden, 3-5 minutes on each side. Remove and keep warm. Add the fresh mushrooms and saute a few minutes. Add the remaining artichoke hearts, the chicken broth, the lemon juice, salt and pepper. Cook a few minutes, pour over chicken breasts and serve.
Serves 4.

 # Almond Chicken

½ cup chicken broth
1½ T. cornstarch
1 egg white
½ tsp. sherry
  flavoring
1 T. honey
½ tsp. Chinese Five
  Spice
3 T. oil
4 chicken breasts,
  cut into pieces
¾ cup blanched
  almonds
3 stalks celery,
  sliced
4 green onions,
  sliced
1 pkg. frozen snow
  peas, barely
  thawed

In a cup stir together the water and cornstarch. Add the egg white, sherry flavoring, honey and Chinese Five Spice. Set aside. In a wok or skillet, heat the oil and then add the chicken and stir-fry until it loses its pink color. Remove chicken from wok or skillet. Add almonds and celery and cook a few minutes. Add green onions and cook a minute more. Return chicken to pan. Add reserved broth mixture and cook until it boils and thickens. Gently stir in snow peas, heat a minute and serve. Good over rice or ramen noodles.
Serves 4-6.

■ Chicken Breasts Scaloppini

Dipping the breasts into Parmesan cheese instead of plain flour helps give this dish its yummy and distinctive taste.

4 boned chicken
  breasts
  Parmesan cheese
2 T. butter or
  margarine
2 T. oil
2 T. flour
1 cup white grape
  juice
1 4 oz. can
  mushrooms, sliced
1 tsp. beef bouillon
½ tsp. herb salt
  dash cayenne
  pepper

Preheat oven to 400°. Pound breasts slightly to flatten. Dip chicken breasts into Parmesan cheese. In a large skillet melt the butter or margarine and add the oil. Heat over medium heat until hot. Saute the chicken breasts briefly, about 3 or 4 minutes on each side. Remove from pan and place in a baking dish. Add the flour to the pan and cook for a few minutes, scraping pan well. Add white grape juice, juice from mushrooms, bouillon, herb salt and cayenne. Cook, stirring constantly until juice thickens. Add mushrooms, heat through and then pour over chicken breasts. Bake about 15 minutes covered, and serve.

Serves 4.

■ Sweet and Sour Chicken Thighs

If it would save time for you to do it this way, you can make up the sauce, pour it over the chicken, and marinate it all in the refrigerator from several hours ahead to early the morning of the day the dish will be cooked.

6 chicken thighs
⅓ cup honey
2 T. lemon juice
1 tsp. Worchester-
  shire sauce
2 T. Dijon mustard

Place chicken thighs in a baking dish. Combine the remaining ingredients. Pour over chicken. Cover and bake at 400° for 30 minutes, basting once. Uncover and baste again. Bake 10 more minutes and serve.

Serves 4-6.

Hungarian Chicken

It is amazing how fast chicken cooks like this on top of the stove. Cooking it in the oven would take much longer.

1 frying chicken, cut up
2 T. butter or margarine
2 T. oil
1 clove garlic, minced
1 cup small onions, peeled—either fresh or frozen ones can be used
2 T. paprika
1½ cups fresh mushrooms
1 16 oz. can tomatoes, chopped
½ cup sour cream or plain yogurt

In a dutch oven or deep heavy skillet melt the butter or margarine and the oil. Brown the pieces of chicken well. Set aside. Add garlic, onions and paprika to oil. Cook for about 2 minutes. Return chicken to pan. Stir to coat with onions and oil in pan. Top with fresh mushrooms and tomatoes. Cover and simmer 20-30 minutes or until chicken is cooked through. Just before serving, stir in sour cream or yogurt.

Serves 4.

Chicken with Water Chestnuts

Light and delicious, this is a classic chicken stir-fried dish.

½ cup chicken broth
2 T. cornstarch
2 T. soy sauce
2 tsp. Chinese Five Spice
3 T. oil
4 chicken breasts, cut into bite size pieces
optional: 1 1-inch piece fresh ginger, finely minced
3 stalks celery, cut into slices
1 onion, cut into wedges and then slices
½ green pepper, sliced
1 pkg. fresh bean sprouts
1 small can water chestnuts

In a cup combine the broth, cornstarch, soy sauce, and Chinese Five Spice. In a wok or skillet place the oil and heat it. Add the chicken breasts and stir-fry until meat loses its pinkness. Remove meat from wok. Add ginger, celery and onions and stir-fry about 3 minutes. Add green pepper and bean sprouts and stir-fry a few more minutes. Add chicken, water chestnuts and the juice. Stir-fry gently until mixture boils and thickens. Good served over rice or ramen noodles.

Serves 4-6.

Italian Chicken

This is good served on top of pasta. A tossed salad and good bread alongside makes a delicious meal.

1 frying chicken, cut up
¼ cup olive oil
1 green pepper, sliced
2 medium onions, sliced
2 small cloves garlic, minced
1 16 oz. can tomatoes, chopped
½ tsp. basil
¼ tsp. oregano
¼ tsp. rosemary
1 can black olives, sliced

In a dutch oven or deep, heavy skillet heat the olive oil. Brown the chicken well in it. Remove. Add the green pepper, onions and garlic. Saute about 3 minutes. Return chicken to pan and stir to coat with onions and oil. Add tomatoes, including juice, and spices. Cover and cook over medium heat 20-30 minutes or until chicken is cooked through. Remove to serving platter and sprinkle olives on top.

Serves 4.

Spicy Chicken with Peanuts

If you don't want your chicken quite so spicy, you can leave out the chili pepper, but it is quite good with it.

½ cup chicken broth
2 T. cornstarch
2 T. soy sauce
2 T. honey
¼ tsp. crushed chili
   pepper
2 T. oil
4 chicken breasts,
   cut into bite size
   pieces
3 carrots, cut into
   slices
5 scallions, cut into
   inch long pieces
⅔ cup peanuts,
   unsalted

In a cup combine the chicken broth, cornstarch, soy sauce, chili pepper, and honey. Set aside. In a wok or large frying pan place the oil and heat it. Stir-fry the pieces of chicken breast, until meat is no longer pink. Remove meat. Stir-fry carrots a few minutes and then add scallions and stir-fry about 1 minute. Return meat to wok or skillet. Add reserved broth mixture and cook, stirring gently until mixture boils and thickens. Good served with rice or ramen noodles.

Serves 4-6.

DESSERTS AND SWEETS

*"Pleasant words are as an honeycomb,
sweet to the soul, and health to the bones."*
—*Proverbs 16:24*

DESSERTS
AND SWEETS

   Desserts don't have to be bad for you to be delicious. Made with honey, whole wheat flour, fresh fruits, nuts and dairy products, the flavor of the recipes below can't be beat. In addition to satisfying your sweet tooth, by using healthful ingredients you are doing more than simply filling your body with empty calories. You're actually building health.

Carob Brownie Pie

Though carob is often known as the natural foods substitute for chocolate, it is a tasty food in its own right. It doesn't contain the harmful caffeine-like substance that chocolate does, nor does it contain the calories of chocolate. It does, however, contain many beneficial trace minerals for your body's health.

½ cup butter or
    margarine,
    softened
¾ cup honey
2 eggs
1 tsp. vanilla
½ cup whole wheat
    pastry flour
3 T. carob powder
¼ tsp. salt
½ cup walnuts,
    chopped

Preheat oven to 350° and grease an 8 inch pie pan. In a medium size mixing bowl beat together the butter or margarine and honey until creamy. Add eggs and vanilla and beat to combine. In another bowl stir together the flour, carob and salt. Add to other mixture and beat a minute or so. Stir in walnuts and pour into pie pan. Bake 20-30 minutes, but watch it carefully so it does not overcook. Remove from oven, cool and cut into wedges. Serve topped with vanilla honey ice cream and Carob Fudge Sauce (below). Additional walnuts can be sprinkled on top.
Serves 6-8.

Carob Banana Sundaes

Carob fudge sauce,
(recipe follows)
honey vanilla ice cream
sliced bananas
chopped nuts
cream whipped with
honey

In individual serving bowls place a few scoops of ice cream. Top with banana slices, carob sauce, nuts and whipped cream.

Carob Fudge Sauce

This rich and creamy sauce is fantastic. Use it in any dish where you would normally use a chocolate sauce.

⅓ cup carob powder
1 tsp. cornstarch
1 5.3 oz. can
   evaporated milk
⅓ cup honey
¼ cup butter
1 tsp. vanilla

Blend the carob powder, cornstarch and the evaporated milk until there are no lumps. It is easy to do this in a blender. Pour this combined mixture into a medium sized saucepan. Add honey and cook over medium heat, stirring constantly until mixture thickens and boils. Remove from heat and stir in butter and vanilla.

Makes about ¾ cup.

Apple Almond Cream

This dessert is perfect for after a ladies' luncheon.

2 apples, cored and
   cubed
2 T. honey
¼ cup toasted,
   chopped almonds
½ cup whipping
   cream
½ tsp. vanilla
¼ tsp. almond
   flavoring
1 T. honey
   additional
   almonds for
   garnish

In a medium size bowl place the apples, honey and almonds. Toss together gently. In another small bowl, beat the cream until soft peaks form. Add the vanilla and almond flavorings and drizzle the additional tablespoon of honey over it. Beat a few more seconds. Fold cream into apple mixture. Place in four serving bowls, top with additional almonds and serve.

Serves 4.

Exotic Fruit Cream

Follow the recipe above, but instead of the apples substitute a combination of fruits such as papaya, strawberries, kiwis, and fresh raspberries. Instead of chopped almonds, substitute chopped macadamia nuts.

 ## Baked Spicy Pears

This is a wonderful dessert for the fall when a hot spicy fruit dish tastes just perfect.

3 cups ripe pears,
   cut into cubes
⅓ cup apple juice
¼ cup water
1 tsp. cornstarch
2 T. honey
1 T. raisins
⅛ tsp. ground
   cinnamon
⅛ tsp. ground mace

Preheat oven to 350°. Place pears in an 8 x 8 inch baking pan. Place the apple juice in a medium size saucepan over medium heat. Stir the cornstarch and water together and add to pan. Add honey, raisins, cinnamon and mace. Cook, stirring constantly until mixture thickens and boils. Pour over pears and bake for 20 to 30 minutes or until pears are fork tender.

Note: Though it would no longer be a low calorie dessert, this is yummy topped with vanilla ice cream or half and half.

Miniature Almond Pound Cakes

These are really yummy. The almond flavor is so good and the topping makes them perfect.

1 cup butter or margarine, softened
½ cup honey
3 eggs
1 tsp. vanilla
1 tsp. almond flavoring
1 8 oz. carton vanilla yogurt
½ cup milk
2 cups whole wheat pastry flour
½ tsp. baking soda
1 tsp. baking powder
½ tsp. salt
¾ cup finely ground almonds
Almond Honey Topping, recipe below

Preheat oven to 350°. Grease well 18 muffin cups. Beat together butter and honey. Add eggs, vanilla, and almond extract and beat. Add yogurt and milk and beat again. In another bowl stir together the flour, soda, baking powder, salt and almonds. Add to liquid mixture and stir to combine. Spoon into muffin cups and bake about 20 minutes or until a toothpick inserted in one comes out clean. Turn out of pan and top with Almond Honey topping.
Serves 18.

Almond Honey Topping

1½ cups honey
¾ cup butter or margarine
½ tsp. almond extract
1 cup sliced almonds

In a small saucepan melt together honey and butter or margarine. Remove from heat and add almond extract and almonds. Allow to cool slightly and spoon over little almond cakes.

Cherry Upside Down Cake

The same type of cake as the ever popular pineapple upside down cake, but with a yummy cherry flavor instead.

⅓ cup butter or margarine, melted
1 16 oz. can black cherries
½ cup honey
¼ cup chopped pecans
¼ cup butter or margarine, softened
½ cup honey
2 eggs
¼ cup milk
2 cups whole wheat pastry flour
1 T. baking powder
½ tsp. salt
Cherry Sauce

Preheat oven to 350°. Grease an 8 x 8 inch baking pan well. Drain juice from black cherries, and reserve it. Place drained cherries and pecans in the pan. In a medium sized mixing bowl, cream together the butter or margarine and honey. Add eggs and milk and beat again. In another bowl stir together the flour, baking powder and salt. Stir dry ingredients into other mixture to combine. Spoon over cherries and pecans. Bake for about 30 minutes or until a toothpick inserted in the top comes out clean. Invert cake, cut into squares and serve with Cherry Sauce spooned on top.

Serves 6-9.

Cherry Sauce

In addition to tasting good on the cake, this sauce is also good over ice cream.

1 16 oz. can black cherries, including juice
juice reserved from can of cherries used in the cake above
3 T. cornstarch
¼ cup water
1 cup honey

In a medium size saucepan place the cherries and the reserved juice. Stir the cornstarch and the water together until smooth. Add this to the pan. Add one cup honey. Stir constantly over medium heat until mixture thickens and boils. Remove from heat, allow to cool slightly and spoon over cherry cake.

Makes about 3 cups.

Honey Nut Popcorn

6 quarts popped
  corn
1½ cups honey
¼ tsp. cinnamon
¼ tsp. orange peel
⅛ tsp. mace
3 T. butter
1 tsp. vanilla
1 cup chopped nuts,
  such as walnuts,
  almonds or
  pecans

Place the popped corn in a large bowl.

In a medium size saucepan with high sides place the honey, cinnamon, orange peel and mace. Bring to a boil and boil for about 10 minutes. Remove from heat and immediately stir in the butter or margarine, vanilla and nuts. Pour over popped corn and stir to coat.

Makes about 12 cups.

Carob Dipped Fruit

1 cup carob morsels
2 T. oil
  fresh strawberries,
  washed and dried
  orange pieces
  pineapple chunks

Melt carob chips over hot, but not boiling, water. Remove from heat, returning if it becomes too cool and thick. Stir in oil (if needed) to thin melted carob. Place orange pieces and pineapple chunks on toothpicks. Dip fruit into carob and place on a foil lined cookie sheet. When all fruit is dipped, refrigerate for 10-15 minutes. Fruit can remain at room temperature for about one hour.

Carob Nut Clusters

These taste just like the candies sold in the natural food stores. They are quick and easy and cost much less to make at home.

1 cup carob morsels
1 cup chopped nuts,
  peanuts, walnuts,
  or whatever you
  desire

Melt carob over hot water. Stir in nuts. Drop onto a cookie sheet. Place in freezer 3-5 minutes or until firm. Remove from cookie sheet.

Makes about 3 dozen pieces.

Yogurt Nut Clusters

1 cup yogurt
  morsels
1 cup chopped nuts,
  peanuts, walnuts,
  or whatever you
  desire.

Melt yogurt morsels over hot water. Stir in nuts. Drop onto a cookie sheet. Place in freezer 3-5 minutes or until firm. Remove from cookie sheet.

Makes about 36 pieces.

Carob or Yogurt Coated Raisins

Follow procedure for the nut clusters, but substitute 1 cup raisins for the nuts.

Watermelon Parfait

2 cups watermelon
  pieces
2 cups fresh
  strawberries, cut
  in half
  fresh lime juice
  optional: fresh
  mint sprigs

In four tall parfait glasses, layer the watermelon and the strawberry pieces. Squeeze fresh lime over each layer. Garnish with fresh mint and serve.

Serves 4.

Iced Pineapple Perfection

2 cups fresh
  pineapple chunks
¼ cup orange juice
¼ cup grated
  coconut
2 cups fresh or
  frozen blueberries

In a small bowl mix together pineapple chunks, orange juice and grated coconut. Place in freezer about half an hour. Remove and mound into sherbet glasses. Garnish with blueberries and serve.

Serves 4.

EGGS

*Those who bring sunshine into the lives of others
cannot keep it from themselves.*

EGGS

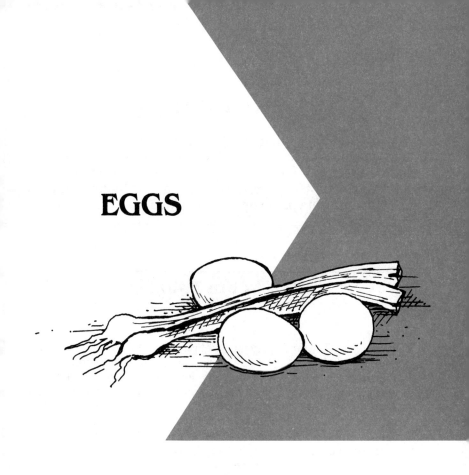

Eggs are considered an almost perfect protein because their protein structure most closely matches the protein structure of our bodies. Two large eggs supply one-third of the body's daily protein needs. Eggs also supply iodine, riboflavin, phosphorus, vitamin D, folic acid, pantothenic acid, vitamin A, iron, zinc, biotin, vitamin B6, thiamin, calcium, copper and magnesium. Quite a nutritious package.

What a variety is available when cooking with eggs—frittatas, omelets, scrambled eggs, eggs with salsa and eggs with cheese—the possibilities are endless. Plus the cost of egg dishes is usually quite low.

Eggs are also extremely quick and easy to prepare. The recipes that follow can be used for breakfasts, lunches, brunches and suppers. If you're in a hurry in your cooking—reach for eggs—you're sure to come out with something delicious.

FRITTATAS

Italian in origin, a frittata is like a quiche cooked on top of the stove without a crust. You can use any variation of vegetables and cheeses in a frittata that you would in a quiche, though many frittatas don't have any cheese in them at all. Try the two variations below to get your imagination started.

Mushroom Frittata

2 T. oil
1 cup fresh mushrooms, sliced
3 green onions, sliced
6-8 eggs
3 T. milk
dash salt and pepper

Place the oil in a 10 inch skillet. Over medium heat, saute the mushrooms and green onions until the mushrooms are tender. In a small bowl, beat together the eggs, milk and dash of salt and pepper. Pour over the mushrooms and onions. Cover pan and cook over low heat until set, 15-20 minutes. Let sit 5 minutes, cut in wedges and serve.
Serves 4-6.

Zucchini Tomato Frittata

2 T. oil
2 zucchini, sliced
1 fresh tomato, sliced
2 green onions, sliced
6-8 eggs
3 T. milk
2 T. Parmesan cheese
½ tsp. basil
dash salt and pepper

Place the oil in a 10 inch skillet. Over medium heat saute the zucchini until barely tender. Add the tomato and green onion and saute a few more minutes. In a small bowl, beat together the eggs, milk, Parmesan cheese, basil and salt and pepper. Pour over vegetables in the skillet. Cover pan and cook over low heat until set, about 15-20 minutes. Let sit 5 minutes, cut in wedges and serve.
Serves 4-6.

Huevos con Avocados

A variation of the popular Huevos Ran-cheros, this dish is yummy served with refried beans and warm flour tortillas.

4 **flour tortillas**
2 **avocados, cut into cubes**
2 **tsp. lemon juice**
4 **poached or fried eggs**
2 **cups mild salsa**
½ **cup grated jack cheese**

Preheat oven to 350°. Fold the flour tortillas in half and place in an approximately 7 x 11 baking dish. In a small bowl, toss together avocados and lemon juice. Spread the avocados over the flour tortillas. Carefully place the poached or fried eggs on top. Spoon salsa over eggs. Sprinkle grated cheese on top. Place in oven for about 7 minutes or until cheese melts.

Serves 4-6.

 # Scrambled Huevos

Using the recipe above, substitute 6 scrambled eggs for the four poached eggs and proceed as directed.

SCRAMBLED SURPRISES

Scrambled eggs are so easy to make and you can do so much with them. The recipes below all combine scrambled eggs in a velvety sauce, which is then spooned over toast, rice, or even a baked potato. The recipes can be made in quantity for a buffet brunch or they make a good, inexpensive and easy entree for a light supper.

■ Shrimp and Mushroom Scrambled Eggs

2 T. butter or
  margarine
1½ T. flour
1 cup milk
  dash salt and
  pepper
¼ tsp. tarragon
6 scrambled eggs
1 6½ oz. can
  shrimp, rinsed
  and drained
1 4 oz. can sliced
  mushrooms,
  drained
  toast, rice, or
  baked potatoes
  enough for 4

In a medium skillet over medium heat, melt the butter or margarine. Add flour and stir, cooking it for a few minutes. Add milk, salt and pepper and cook, stirring constantly until thickened. Add tarragon, scrambled eggs, shrimp and mushrooms. Stir gently until heated through. Serve over toast, rice or a baked potato.

Serves 4.

■ ❖ Eggs, Spinach and Potato Supper

This is really yummy and very hearty. It can be served as a vegetarian main dish or it makes a satisfying side dish for a hungry group when served with a meat entree and salad.

3 T. olive oil
1 small onion,
  chopped
2 cloves garlic,
  chopped
3 medium potatoes,
  cubed
3 cups fresh
  spinach, chopped
5 eggs
  dash salt and
  pepper
¼ cup grated jack or
  Parmesan cheese

In a large skillet over medium heat place the olive oil, onion, garlic and potatoes. Cover and cook for about 20 minutes, or until potatoes are barely tender, stirring every few minutes. At the end of that time, remove the lid. Beat eggs with salt and pepper. Add eggs and spinach to mixture. Stir gently, continuing to cook until eggs are set and spinach is wilted. Top with grated cheese, replace lid for 5 minutes and serve. This is especially good with a fresh tomato salad.

Serves 6.

Eggs and Chicken Livers

½ cup beef broth
½ cup chicken livers, cut into small pieces
2 T. butter or margarine
3 green onions, chopped
2 T. butter or margarine
1½ T. flour
1 cup milk
dash salt and pepper
6 eggs, scrambled toast, rice or baked potatoes for four

In a small skillet place the beef broth and chicken livers. Heat slowly until chicken livers are cooked. Drain broth. Cut up livers. In another skillet, melt the 2 tablespoons butter or margarine and cook the green onions briefly, about 5 minutes, then add the chicken livers and cook a few more minutes. In another skillet, melt the other 2 tablespoons butter or margarine, stir in the flour, and cook for a few minutes over medium heat. Add the milk and cook, stirring constantly until thickened. Add salt and pepper, chicken livers, onion mixture and the scrambled eggs. Spoon over toast, rice or baked potoatoes.
Serves 4.

 # Scrambled Eggs with Green Onions and Almonds

3 T. butter or margarine
3 green onions
2 T. flour
1 cup milk
dash salt and pepper
½ cup sliced almonds
6 scrambled eggs toast, rice or baked potatoes for four

In a medium skillet over medium heat, melt the butter or margarine. Add the green onions and cook a few minutes. Add the flour and cook a few more minutes. Add the milk and cook, stirring constantly until thickened. Add the salt and pepper, almonds, and scrambled eggs. Serve over toast, rice or baked potoatoes.
Serves 4.

FISH

*"O taste and see that the Lord is good:
blessed is the man that trusteth in him."*
—*Psalm 34:8*

FISH

Fish by its very nature is quick and easy to prepare. It cooks in a short period of time and care should always be taken to never overcook it. Because fish is low in fat, it is also low in calories, making it a good food for those on diets.

Though fresh fish is always delicious, you do not need fresh, expensive varieties of fish for the recipes in this section. They were all made with frozen fish available in any supermarket year round. The proper cooking methods and seasonings are what make delicious cooked fish, not the price tag on it.

Shrimp Topped Fish

Very nice in appearance, this makes a nice company dish and is liked even by my friends "who don't like fish."

1 10 oz. pkg. frozen spinach, thawed
1 lb. white fish pieces such as turbot or sole
1 6½ oz. can shrimp pieces, rinsed and drained
2 T. green onion, chopped
2 T. Parmesan cheese
   dash salt and pepper
½ cup carbonated white grape juice
2 T. lemon juice

Preheat oven to 350°. In a 9 x 13 baking dish place the spinach on the bottom. Lay the pieces of fish on top. In a small bowl combine the shrimp pieces, green onion, Parmesan cheese, salt and pepper. Spoon over the fish. Pour grape juice and lemon juice over fish. Cover and bake for about 30 minutes or until fish flakes.

Serves 4.

Oven Barbecued Fish

1 lb. perch
1 4 oz. can tomato paste
¼ cup Worcester-shire sauce
2 T. honey
¼ tsp. cayenne pepper
1 T. mustard
1 T. green onion, finely chopped
   dash salt and pepper

Lay pieces of perch in baking dish. Combine tomato paste, Worcestershire sauce, honey, cayenne pepper, mustard, green onion, salt and pepper. Spoon over fish. Place in a 400° oven, cook for 5 minutes uncovered, turn and baste. Cook for 5-10 minutes more or until fish flakes.

Serves 4.

Cheesy Sole Florentine

2 10 oz. pkgs. frozen spinach, thawed
1 lb. sole
2 T. butter or margarine
2 T. flour
½ cup chicken broth or bouillon
½ cup half and half
¾ cup grated Swiss cheese
1 tsp. Dijon mustard
dash salt and pepper
paprika

In a 9 x 13 baking dish place the spinach. Lay pieces of sole on top. In a medium saucepan over medium heat melt the butter or margarine, stir in flour and cook a minute or two. Add chicken broth and half and half and cook, stirring constantly until it thickens. Add Swiss cheese and melt into sauce. Season with mustard, salt and pepper. Pour over fish. Sprinkle on paprika for garnish. Bake in 375° oven covered, about 30 minutes or until fish flakes.

Serves 4.

 ## Fish Fillets with Butter Parsley Sauce

This is a very light and refreshing sauce for fish.

1 lb. white fish fillets such as sole or turbot
flour, salt and pepper
3 T. butter
juice of ½ lemon
1 T. parsley

Wipe fish dry, then dip into mixture of flour, salt and pepper. In a large skillet melt the butter. Saute fish pieces briefly, about 3 minutes on each side or until golden and cooked through. Remove from pan and keep warm. Add lemon to pan. Stir, scraping sides and bottom. Add parsley, stir one minute and pour over fish fillets. Serve immediately.

Serves 4.

Fish Fillets Almondine

This is one of my favorite ways to prepare inexpensive fish. It's easy, but special enough for company.

1 lb. white fish
  fillets such as
  sole or turbot
  flour, salt and
  pepper
3 T. butter
¼ cup carbonated
  white grape juice
⅓ cup sliced
  almonds

Wipe fish dry and then dip into mixture of flour, salt and pepper. In a large skillet melt the butter. Add the pieces of fish and saute on each side about 3 minutes or until golden and cooked through. Remove from pan and set aside. Add white grape juice and stir, scraping sides and bottom. Add almonds and cook a minute. Spoon over fish and serve.

Serves 4.

Fish Fillets with Mushroom Sauce

The sauce is elegant, rich and creamy. Save this dish for special occasions.

Sauce:
2 tsp. butter or
  margarine
2 tsp. flour
½ cup chicken broth
½ cup half and half
1 can chopped
  shrimp, rinsed and
  drained
1 can mushrooms,
  chopped

2 lbs. white fish
  fillets
  flour
3 T. butter
  Parmesan cheese
  paprika

Preheat oven to 375°. Make sauce first. In a medium skillet over medium heat melt the butter or margarine. Add flour and cook a minute or so. Add the chicken broth and half and half. Cook, stirring constantly until thickened. Add shrimp and mushrooms. Set sauce aside.

Pat fish dry and dip into flour. In a large skillet melt butter and saute fish about three minutes on each side or until golden and cooked through. Place fish in a 9 x 13 baking dish. Pour sauce over. Sprinkle a little Parmesan cheese and a bit of paprika on top. Heat for about 5-10 minutes or until sauce is hot and bubbly. Serve immediately.

Serves 6-8.

Fennel Flavored Fish Stew

Fennel is a licorice flavored spice that makes an unusual and tasty complement to fish.

¼ cup olive oil
½ tsp. fennel seed
3 cloves garlic,
  finely minced
1 onion, finely
  chopped
1 stalk celery,
  chopped
1 16 oz. can
  tomatoes,
  chopped
8 cups water
4 red boiling
  potatoes,
  unpeeled and
  sliced thin
2 lbs. white fish cut
  into chunks
1 T. parsley flakes
1 bay leaf
½ tsp. orange peel
¼ tsp. dried thyme
  dash salt and
  pepper

In the bottom of a large soup pot place the olive oil, fennel, onion, garlic and celery. Saute until onions are soft. Add tomatoes, water and potatoes. Bring to a boil and boil about 10 minutes. Add fish and remaining seasonings. Turn down heat and simmer about 15 minutes or until fish flakes.

Serves 6-8.

Lemon Baked Fish

The delicate herb and lemon flavor in this recipe works well with fresh fish though frozen fish works fine also.

1 lb. white fish fillets
juice of one lemon
1 T. parsley flakes
¼ tsp. dill
¼ tsp. tarragon
¼ tsp. chervil
1 lemon, thinly sliced
1 T. butter or margarine
paprika

Preheat oven to 325°. In a 9 × 13 baking dish arrange the fish slices. Pour lemon juice over them. In a small bowl combine the parsley flakes, dill, tarragon and chervil. Sprinkle on fish. Top fish with sliced lemon. Dot on butter or margarine. Sprinkle paprika on top. Bake for about 20 minutes or until fish flakes.
Serves 4.

Stir-Fried Scallops

If you purchase the large scallops, cut them in slices. Sometimes you can find miniature scallops in the store. They are usually cheaper and are perfect for this recipe.

½ cup chicken broth
2 tsp. honey
1 tsp. Chinese Five Spice
2 tsp. cornstarch
2 T. oil
1 lb. scallops, sliced
½ cup celery, sliced
⅓ cup green onions, sliced
1 small can water chestnuts, sliced
2 pkgs. snow peas, thawed

In a cup stir together the chicken broth, honey, Chinese Five Spice, and cornstarch. In a wok or large skillet heat the oil. Add the scallops and stir-fry until cooked. Remove. Add the celery and green onion and stir-fry briefly. Add water chestnuts, snow peas, scallops and broth mixture. Cook, stirring gently until mixture thickens.
Serves 4.

Red Clam Chowder

A delicious variation of the traditional clam chowder.

¼ cup olive oil
½ onion, chopped
2 stalks celery, sliced
2 carrots, sliced
1 16 oz. can tomatoes, chopped
3 cups water
2 cups clam juice
4 potatoes, cubed
1 6 oz. can tomato paste
2 cans clams, juice included
¼ tsp. thyme
¼ tsp. oregano
   salt and pepper

In the bottom of a large kettle place the olive oil, onion, celery and carrots. Saute about 5 minutes. Add tomatoes, water, clam juice and potatoes. Heat to a boil and boil about 15 minutes or until potatoes are tender. Add tomato paste, clams, thyme and oregano. Heat through.
   Serves 6-8.

Sole Veronique

1 lb. sole
   herb salt
2 T. butter
2 T. flour
½ cup chicken broth
½ cup half and half
¼ tsp. thyme
1 cup seedless green grapes
   paprika
1 lemon, sliced

Preheat oven to 375°. Lay pieces of sole in a 9 x 13 baking dish. Sprinkle with herb salt. In a medium skillet melt the butter. Add flour and stir, cooking for a few minutes. Add chicken broth, half and half, and thyme. Cook, stirring constantly until thickened. Add one cup seedless green grapes. Heat through a couple of minutes. Spoon over fish fillets and bake covered for about 20-30 minutes or until fish flakes. Remove. Garnish with lemon slices and paprika and serve.
   Serves 4.

Stir-Fried Shrimp and Broccoli

Not only does this taste great, but it also looks delicious.

½ cup chicken broth
1 T. honey
2 T. soy sauce
2 tsp. cornstarch
¼ cup oil
1 tsp. fresh ginger, grated
1 lb. fresh or frozen shrimp
1 cup frozen broccoli pieces, thawed
1 4 oz. can button mushrooms, drained
1 can sliced bamboo shoots, drained

In a cup stir together the chicken broth, honey, soy sauce and cornstarch. In a wok or large frying pan place the oil and heat. Add fresh ginger and shrimp. Stir-fry shrimp until done. Add broccoli pieces, mushrooms and bamboo shoots. Stir-fry gently a few minutes to heat through. Add chicken broth mixture and heat until mixture thickens. Serve over rice or noodles.

Serves 4.

PASTA

Today well lived makes every yesterday a dream of happiness and every tomorrow a vision of hope.

PASTA

If you want a meal that is quick and delicious, you can't beat pasta. And, with over 500 varieties to choose from, you'll never be bored. You can choose all sorts of shapes from shells to spaghetti, and all kinds of pasta from spinach to sesame. If you haven't tried some of the different varieties, experiment. You're sure to find some new favorites.

While you are experimenting, try some of the pasta varieties at your natural food store or section of your grocery. There you will find sesame, whole wheat and various vegetable based pastas—all of which are usually more healthful than the plain, white flour variety.

Do a little experimenting when you cook these pastas because the time needed to cook the various varieties may be different than what you are normally used to. When cooking any pasta, use at least 3 times the amount of water than you have pasta and cook in a pot that the water and pasta can boil freely in without boiling over. Add 2 teaspoons of salt and one tablespoon of oil to the cooking water to keep the pasta from sticking together while it cooks.

The most important thing to remember when cooking pasta is not to overcook it. You want your noodles still chewy and never mushy.

One fun entertainment idea with pasta is to cook a big batch of pasta, and about 3 or 4 various kinds of sauces. Serve it buffet style and allow your guests to sample the different sauces. Accompanied by a big tossed salad and lots of French bread, you have the makings of a wonderful time.

Fresh Mushroom Sauce

One of everybody's favorite sauces.

¼ **cup olive oil**
2 **cloves garlic,**
   crushed
¼ **cup onion,**
   chopped
4 **cups fresh**
   mushrooms, sliced
   in half
2 **8 oz. cans tomato**
   sauce
½ **tsp. basil**
   salt and pepper

In a large saucepan saute the garlic and onions a few minutes. Add the mushrooms and saute briefly. Add tomato sauce, basil, salt and pepper. Simmer 10 minutes.

Makes about 4 cups.

Broccoli and Pine Nut Sauce

2 **T. olive oil**
½ **onion, finely**
   chopped
2 **cloves garlic,**
   mashed
1 **cup chicken broth**
1 **16 oz. pkg. frozen**
   chopped broccoli,
   thawed
¼ **cup pine nuts**

In a medium skillet saute the onions and garlic in the olive oil briefly. Add chicken broth, broccoli and pine nuts. Heat through and serve.

Makes about 2½ cups.

Walnut Sauce

A rather exotic, rich and creamy sauce.

½ cup olive oil
1 clove garlic, crushed
1 cup chopped walnuts
1 cup cream
½ tsp. marjoram

In a medium skillet heat the olive oil and the garlic together over medium heat for 2 minutes. Add the walnuts and heat 2 more minutes. Add the cream and marjoram and heat through.

Makes about 1 cup.

White Clam Sauce

This is really a yummy sauce and one of my favorites. It is especially nice served over spinach pasta.

½ cup butter
2 cloves garlic, minced
3 green onions, chopped
1 T. flour
½ cup chicken broth
2 6½ oz. cans clams, juice included
2 T. chopped fresh parsley
salt and pepper to taste

In a medium saucepan melt the butter. Saute the garlic and onions for a couple of minutes. Stir the flour in and cook a few more minutes. Add chicken broth and clams, including juice, to skillet. Cook, stirring frequently until slightly thickened. Add parsley, salt and pepper.

Makes about 1½ cups.

Red Clam Sauce

Some people prefer all their pasta sauces to have a tomato base. This is the clam sauce for them.

3 T. olive oil
2 cloves garlic, minced
½ onion, chopped
1 6½ oz. can clams with juice
1 8 oz. can tomato sauce
salt and pepper

In a medium saucepan over medium heat place the oil, garlic and onion. Saute until soft. Add clams, tomato sauce, salt and pepper and heat through.

Makes about 1 cup.

Tuscany Bean Sauce

This is rather different in taste, but really good. It is my adaptation of an original Northern Italian recipe. A missionary friend of mine from Italy assured me that this is the sort of pasta sauce eaten today among the poorer peoples. What they may lack in material resources, they do know how to make up for in taste.

3 T. olive oil
2 cloves garlic, minced
½ tsp. sage
1 16 oz. can tomatoes, chopped
1 16 oz. can white beans

In a medium size pan over medium heat saute the garlic in the olive oil a few minutes. Add the sage, tomatoes, and white beans and simmer about 20 minutes.

Makes about 2 cups.

Zucchini Tomato Sauce

I like to make up a large amount of this and freeze it in the summer when fresh tomatoes and zucchini are available in abundance.

2 T. olive oil
1 clove garlic, chopped
½ onion, chopped
3 zucchini, sliced
3 fresh tomatoes, in chunks
1 8 oz. can tomato sauce
½ tsp. basil
¼ tsp. oregano

In a large skillet heat the olive oil. Add the garlic and onions and saute a few minutes. Add the zucchini and tomatoes and saute until zucchini is barely tender. Add tomato sauce, basil and oregano. Simmer about 10 minutes.

Makes about 3½ cups.

Prima Vera Sauce

Often made with steamed fresh vegetables, by using frozen ones this becomes a very quick version while still retaining basic taste.

2 T. butter
2 cloves garlic, minced
1 T. flour
2 cups half and half
1 cup Parmesan cheese
1 16 oz. pkg. fancy, frozen vegetables (such as Italian or Florentine), thawed by running warm water over them
½ tsp. basil

In a large skillet melt the butter. Add the garlic and saute a minute. Add the flour and cook a few minutes. Add the half and half and cook, stirring gently until it thickens slightly. Add the Parmesan cheese and stir to dissolve. Add the package of frozen vegetables and basil and simmer about 10 minutes.

Makes about 4 cups.

Pesto

Fresh basil is hard to find, but it isn't very hard to grow in your own garden. If you do, make up large batches of this. It freezes nicely and you will have a very special treat available all year.

2 **cups fresh basil**
4 **cloves garlic**
1 **cup grated Parmesan cheese**
¼ **cup olive oil**
¼ **cup melted butter**
¼ **cup walnuts**

Puree all ingredients in a food processor or blender.

Makes about 1 cup.

Whole Wheat Macaroni and Cheese

1 **cup whole wheat elbow noodles**
2 **T. oil**
½ **onion, chopped**
1 **clove garlic, minced**
3 **tomatoes, cut up**
2 **T. butter or margarine**
2 **T. flour**
1½ **cups milk**
1 **cup grated cheddar cheese**
¼ **cup grated cheddar cheese**

Preheat oven to 350°. Cook whole wheat noodles and drain; set aside. In a medium size saucepan place the oil. Add garlic and onions and saute until tender. Add tomatoes and saute a minute or two. Mix onion, garlic and tomatoes with noodles. In the same pan melt the butter or margarine. Add the flour and cook a few minutes, stirring constantly. Add milk and cook until it begins to thicken. Stir in grated cheddar cheese. Place noodle mixture in a baking dish and stir in cheese sauce. Top with remaining ¼ cup shredded cheese. Bake about 10 minutes or until hot and bubbly.

Serves 4-6.

Fettucini with Crab

Absolutely elegant, fettucini is one of the nicest ways to prepare pasta. Serve it for a special company dinner.

4 eggs, beaten
1½ cups half and half
1 lb. fettucini
noodles
½ cup melted butter
1 cup fresh
mushrooms, thinly
sliced
1 cup grated
Parmesan cheese
1 small can crab,
drained
dash salt and
pepper

Set out eggs and half and half. Allow to come to room temperature. Mix together melted butter, mushrooms, salt and pepper. Set aside and keep warm. Cook fettucini noodles according to package directions. A few minutes before they are done, place serving platter in the oven to warm. When fettucini is cooked, remove the platter and place drained fettucini on it. Toss with eggs, half and half and butter. Add mushrooms, crab, salt and pepper mixture and toss again with grated cheese. Serve immediately.

Serves 6.

Fettucini with Shrimp

Follow recipe above but substitute 1 can shrimp or ½ pound thawed, frozen shrimp for the crab.

Fettucini with Asparagus and Mushrooms

Follow recipe above but substitute 1 10 oz. package frozen asparagus tips that are cooked and hot for the crab.

SALADS

Some pursue happiness—others create it.

SALADS

Variety is the spice of life we are told, and nowhere is this more true than in our diets. The same foods day after day, week after week, no matter how good they are, after a while can become tasteless and boring. In addition to fighting sheer boredom, nutritionists tell us that a varied diet is the best way to insure that we are getting all the nutrients we need for proper health.

Unfortunately, our diet imaginations fail us most often in the area of salads. Iceburg lettuce, a few pieces of tomato, maybe carrot slivers and a mushroom if we are feeling particularly adventurous, is the standard composition of our salads. Though a salad like that can be very good, we are missing out on an abundance of riches if we stop there.

Just the lettuce itself can be varied in so many ways. Remember the rule that the darker the green in the lettuce the higher the vitamin content. Try romaine, leaf, butter and endive lettuce instead of the old standby of iceburg. Add different ingredients to a basic tossed salad: cheese, nuts, different sorts of vegetables.

Another area that can be varied wonderfully is salad dressings. Most commercial dressings are overpriced and full of sugar and artificial colorings and flavorings. Making your own dressing is easy and the results are fantastic. In addition you control all that goes into them and you can adjust the amount of sweetness or salt in the final product.

Artichoke Lettuce Salad

This is especially good when served with Italian foods such as lasagna and pasta. It also goes well with tomato flavored meat dishes such as the Chicken Tosca, page 76.

1 6 oz. can
artichoke hearts,
juice included
¼ cup lemon juice
2 T. honey
¼ tsp. lemon pepper
1 cup frozen peas,
thawed by running
warm water over
them briefly
1 cup chopped
celery
3 cups endive, torn
in pieces
3 cups green leaf
lettuce, torn in
pieces

Cut artichoke hearts in pieces and place them in the bottom of a large salad bowl. Place the lemon juice, honey, and lemon pepper on top and stir mixture together. Place peas and celery on top. Place endive and leaf lettuce on top of this. It can be covered and chilled at this point until ready to serve, or it can be tossed and served immediately.

Serves 4.

Creamy Pear Salad

To make sure your pears are ripe enough, purchase them several days ahead and store at room temperature in a paper bag.

6 ripe pears, peeled
and sliced
¼ cup sour cream
¼ cup plain yogurt
⅓ cup honey
dash cinnamon
dash nutmeg

Place pears in serving bowl. Combine sour cream, yogurt, honey, cinnamon and nutmeg. Gently stir into pears and serve.

Serves 4.

Cucumber Lettuce Salad

This is a very refreshing salad that goes well with hearty main dishes.

½ **head iceburg lettuce, cleaned and torn into bite size pieces**
2 **cucumbers, peeled and sliced**
2 **zucchini, cleaned and sliced**
2 **green onions, chopped Cucumber Dressing p. 133.**

In a large bowl place the lettuce, cucumbers, zucchini and onions. Add the Cucumber Dressing. Toss and serve.
Serves 6.

Mexican Salad

This is a great salad to serve with a buffet of Mexican foods.

1 **head iceberg lettuce, torn into pieces**
1 **16 oz. can kidney beans**
1 **small bag corn or tortilla chips**
¾ **cup mayonnaise**
¼ **cup salsa**
1 **tsp. chili powder, more or less to taste**
¼ **tsp. cumin**

In a large bowl place the lettuce, kidney beans and corn or tortilla chips. In a small bowl stir together the mayonnaise, salsa, chili powder and cumin. Pour the dressing over the lettuce mixture and toss to combine and serve.
Serves 6.

Tomatoes with Fresh Basil

Though fresh basil is sometimes hard to find, the unforgettable flavor of this salad makes it worth it.

4 ripe tomatoes, sliced
1½ tsp. fresh basil, chopped
1 T. white wine vinegar
4 T. olive oil
½ clove garlic, chopped very fine
  dash salt and pepper

Arrange tomato slices on serving plate. Sprinkle fresh basil over the tomatoes. In a cup combine the vinegar, olive oil, garlic and salt and pepper. Pour over the tomato slices and serve.

Note: You can make this into a low calorie salad by omitting the olive oil and following the remainder of the recipe.
Serves 4.

Banana Nut Salad

4 bananas, peeled and sliced
¼ cup lemon juice
2 cups seedless green grapes
1 cup walnuts, chopped
½ cup vanilla yogurt
1 T. maple syrup
  lettuce

In a medium bowl place the bananas. Toss with lemon juice. Add green grapes and walnuts. Carefully stir in vanilla yogurt and maple syrup. Serve over lettuce leaves.
Serves 4.

Cucumber Tomato Salad

This salad is good with ground beef en-trees, such as the varieties of baked burgers, page 27.

2 cucumbers, peeled
   and sliced
2 tomatoes,
   chopped
2 green onions,
   chopped
   Spicy Vinaigrette
   Dressing, p. 134.

In a medium bowl, place the cucumbers, tomatoes, and green onions. Pour the Spicy Vinaigrette Dressing over and toss gently. Serves 4.

 ## Walnut and Avocado Salad

2 ripe avocados, cut
   into pieces
2 apples, cored and
   cut into pieces
2 T. lemon juice
¼ cup walnuts,
   chopped
   Basic Honey
   French Dressing,
   p. 132.

In a medium size bowl place the avocado and apple pieces. Toss lightly with the lemon juice. Gently stir in the walnuts. Add the Basic Honey French Dressing, toss again and serve. Serves 4.

Fancy Fruit Salad

A unique and delicious combination of flavors, this salad also looks lovely when served.

2 avocados, peeled
   and sliced
2 T. lemon juice
1 grapefruit, peeled
   and cut into slices
1 cup fresh
   strawberries
¼ cup sliced
   almonds or pinon
   nuts
   Fancy Fruit
   Dressing, p. 134.

In a small bowl gently toss together the avocado and the lemon juice. On a serving platter arrange the avocados, grapefruit and strawberries. Pour Fancy Fruit Dressing over and garnish with sliced almonds or pinon nuts.
   Serves 6.

Spinach Orange Salad

2 cups fresh
   spinach leaves,
   torn into small
   pieces
2 oranges, peeled
   and cut into
   chunks
   optional: 1 cup
   fresh strawberries
   Poppy Seed
   Dressing, p. 136.

In a medium bowl place the spinach leaves, the oranges and the strawberries if desired. Add the Poppy Seed Dressing and toss.
   Serves 4.

Romaine Roquefort Salad

This salad has a very sophisticated taste, yet it is one many people enjoy. This is a good salad to serve at a nice dinner party.

½ head romaine lettuce, torn in pieces
½ head green leaf lettuce, torn in pieces
⅓ cup roquefort or blue cheese, crumbled
¼ cup walnuts, chopped
1 cup fresh mushrooms, sliced
Walnut Oil Dressing, p. 134.

In a large bowl place the romaine lettuce, leaf lettuce, cheese, walnuts and mushrooms. Toss with Walnut Oil Dressing.

Serves 6.

Cauliflower Salad

In addition to tasting good, the black and white contrast of colors in this salad is striking.

2 cups frozen cauliflower pieces
2 sticks celery, sliced
2 green onions, sliced
1 4½ oz. can sliced black olives
3 T. capers
Spicy Vinaigrette Dressing, p. 134.

Place frozen cauliflower in a colander and run under hot water until thawed. Run cold water over it a minute to chill it. Place in a medium bowl and add celery, onions, black olives and capers. Pour Spicy Vinaigrette Dressing over it and toss.

Serves 4.

Kiwi Citrus Salad

Kiwis are a wonderful fruit. Though they originated in New Zealand they are now being grown in California. They are delicious, with a taste that one friend described as being "like a green strawberry." They are high in fiber and vitamin C and low in calories.

3 kiwis, peeled and sliced
2 oranges, peeled and cubed
2 tangerines, peeled and cubed
Poppy Seed Dressing, p. 136.

In a medium bowl place the kiwis, oranges and tangerines. Pour the Poppy Seed Dressing over and toss gently to coat.
Serves 4.

Nutty Fruit Salad

The peanut dressing is a surprisingly delicious partner with fruit in this salad.

1 apple, chopped
2 bananas, sliced
2 T. lemon juice
1 cup green grapes
2 oranges, cut into chunks
¼ cup raw peanuts, chopped
Peanut Butter Dressing, p. 135.

In a medium bowl place apples and banana. Gently toss with the lemon juice. Add the remaining fruit. Gently toss with the Peanut Dressing. Sprinkle on chopped peanuts for garnish.
Serves 4.

Greek Salad

Serve this salad on a very large platter. You want all the ingredients to show, so you don't want to have to pile them very deep. It is a wonderful buffet salad.

1 head green leaf
   lettuce, torn in
   pieces
1 cup cherry
   tomatoes, cut in
   half
1 cucumber, peeled
   and cut in slices
3 green onions,
   chopped
¼ cup black Greek
   olives
¼ cup green Greek
   olives
½ cup feta cheese,
   in pieces
6 radishes, sliced
1 T. capers
   Greek
   Vinaigrette
   Dressing, p. 133.

On a large serving platter place the lettuce leaves. Scatter the remaining ingredients over them. Just before serving add the Greek Vinaigrette Dressing.

Serves 8-10.

 # Endive, Orange and Walnut Salad

This is a very colorful as well as tasty salad.

4 cups endive, torn
   in pieces
2 oranges, cut up
¼ cup walnuts
   Lemon Honey
   Dressing p. 133.

In a large bowl toss together the endive, oranges and walnuts. Toss again with Lemon Honey Dressing, page 133, and serve.

Serves 4.

SALAD DRESSINGS

Making your own dressings is fun, easy and economical. It is also the best way to guarantee dressings that are free from chemical additives and full of healthy ingredients. The delicious flavor of homemade dressing is unlike anything that could ever come from a bottle.

Vinegar and oil are the basic ingredients in many dressings. Today there are numerous sorts of oils and vinegars available. Safflower, sunflower, olive and sesame oil from a natural food store all make delicious dressings. Special nut oils such as walnut are also now available and make delicious dressings.

In addition to the old standbys of cider vinegar and wine vinegar, many new sorts of vinegars are also now available. Balsamic vinegar is one of the best and there are numerous flavored vinegars, from raspberry to tarragon, that you can also try.

The recipes for the dressings below will taste yummy with the simplest of ingredients, but feel free if you wish to experiment with some more exotic varieties. You're sure to be happy with the results.

Some of the recipes below were created for specific salads in the previous section, but they can be used with any other tossed or fruit salad of your choice.

✿ Basic Honey French Dressing

This is a good, all purpose basic dressing for green, tossed salads. If you don't know what else to use, you can't go wrong with this one.

⅓ cup vinegar
⅓ cup oil
2 T. honey
1 clove garlic, crushed
¼ tsp. dry mustard
    salt and pepper

Combine ingredients until well blended.

Variation: for the red, "catalina" style French dressing, add to the recipe above ⅓ cup catsup, 1 more tablespoon of honey and ¼ teaspoon celery seed.

Makes about ⅔ cup.

Cucumber Herb Dressing

Similar to the "ranch" style commercial dressings.

1 **cup mayonnaise or plain yogurt**
½ **cup buttermilk**
½ **cucumber, peeled, seeded and chopped**
½ **tsp. dried parsley**
¼ **tsp. garlic powder**
¼ **tsp. dill**
¼ **tsp. marjoram dash each of tarragon, basil, salt and pepper**

Place all ingredients in a food processor or blender and combine.
Makes about 1 cup.

✼ Lemon Honey Dressing

¼ **cup fresh lemon juice**
⅓ **cup oil**
2 **T. honey**
1 **tsp. grated lemon peel optional: for a spicier taste, add 1 T. mustard**

Combine all ingredients. Serve over a tossed salad.
Makes about ½ cup.

Greek Vinaigrette Dressing

⅔ **cup olive oil**
⅓ **cup white wine vinegar**
1 **tsp. oregano**
⅛ **tsp. dried mint**

Combine all ingredients well.
Makes about 1 cup.

Fancy Fruit Dressing

This is not only delicious, but it comes out a very pretty pink color that looks beautiful on fruit salads.

½ **cup mayonnaise**
¼ **cup sour cream or plain yogurt**
¼ **cup honey**
¼ **tsp. dried mint**
¼ **tsp. orange extract**
½ **cup strawberries, fresh or frozen**

Combine all ingredients in a food processor or blender until well mixed. Serve over fruit salad.

Makes about 1 cup.

Walnut Oil Dressing

⅔ **cup walnut oil**
⅓ **cup red wine vinegar**
1 **tsp. Dijon style mustard**
2 **T. honey dash salt and pepper**

Combine all ingredients well.
Makes about 1 cup.

Spicy Vinaigrette Dressing

⅔ **cup oil**
⅓ **cup vinegar**
2 **T. honey**
1 **T. Dijon mustard dash cayenne pepper dash salt and pepper**

Combine all ingredients well.
Makes about 1 cup.

✤ Egg and Oil Dressing

Though the ingredients used are a little unusual, the taste is quite good. You can't tell there are eggs in the dressing, but they give it a creamy, smooth taste as well as adding additional protein to the dressing.

²⁄₃ cup oil
¹⁄₃ cup vinegar
1 tsp. honey
1 hardboiled egg, chopped fine
1 T. green onion, chopped very fine
dash salt and pepper

Combine all ingredients in a blender or food processor.
Makes about 1 cup.

Peanut Butter Dressing

¹⁄₃ cup lemon juice
¼ cup honey
²⁄₃ cup raw peanut butter

Combine all ingredients in a food processor or blender.
Makes about 1 cup.

Yogurt Blue Cheese Dressing

Classic blue cheese dressing made the healthy way. The thickness can be adjusted by varying the amount of milk added to it.

½ cup plain yogurt
½ cup mayonnaise
¼ cup milk
¼ cup blue cheese, crumbled
¼ tsp. garlic powder
dash salt and pepper

Combine ingredients well.
Makes about 1¼ cup.

Sweet Yogurt Dressing

1 cup plain yogurt
¼ cup real maple
   syrup
½ tsp. cinnamon
½ tsp. nutmeg

Combine all ingredients.
Makes about 1 cup.

 ## Poppy Seed Dressing

*This seems to be everybody's all time
favorite dressing. It is great with fruit salads.
Tossed salads that feature some fruit or
avocado also work well with it.*

⅓ cup vinegar
⅔ cup oil
⅓ cup honey
2 T. poppy seeds

Combine all ingredients well. Use a food
processor or blender if possible.
Makes about 1¼ cups.

SANDWICHES

What time is it?
Time to do well,
Time to live better,
Give up that grudge,
Answer that letter,
Speak the kind word to sweeten a sorrow,
Do that kind deed you would leave 'till tomorrow.
—Anonymous: What Time Is It?

SANDWICHES

We all know sandwiches are quick to make, but often they are boring and not too healthy. They don't have to be either.

Like any other recipe, it all depends on the ingredients that go into the final product. If you use white bread and luncheon meat with lots of preservatives or artificial peanut butter and sugary jam, of course you will end up with a sandwich that isn't very healthful.

On the other hand, if you use whole wheat bread, natural cheeses, good meats like turkey and top that off with sprouts, you'll have a sandwich that doesn't take any longer to prepare, and is much better for you.

Have fun with the sandwich recipes that follow. Some are quite out of the ordinary, but they are all delicious.

Turkey with Blue Cheese

Try this with Thanksgiving leftovers for something different.

slices of turkey
slices of blue cheese
  (Stilton is the best,
  but any kind will do)
Dijon mustard
mayonnaise
lettuce
whole wheat bread

Spread one slice of wheat bread with mustard, one with mayonnaise. Arrange slices of turkey and blue cheese on bread. Add lettuce and serve.

Hot Shrimp Sandwich

This is a nice sandwich to serve for a special luncheon.

1 6½ oz. can shrimp
  pieces
¼ cup celery, diced
  fine
1 T. green onion,
  chopped
2 T. French dressing
¼ cup mayonnaise
  dash chili powder
8 slices whole
  wheat bread
3 beaten eggs
1 T. milk
¼ cup butter or
  margarine

In a small bowl mix together the shrimp pieces, celery, green onion, French dressing, mayonnaise and chili powder. Spread on 4 slices of the whole wheat bread to make four sandwiches. Stir together beaten egg and milk and place in a shallow bowl. Dip sandwiches into egg mixture and cook in melted butter or margarine over medium heat until lightly brown on each side.
Serves 4.

Fried Mozzarella and Tomato

This sandwich is a new twist on the old grilled cheese sandwich.

8 slices whole
  wheat bread
4 slices mozzarella
  cheese
4 slices tomato
½ tsp. basil
2 eggs, beaten
¼ cup milk
  oil for frying

Lay out four slices of the whole wheat bread. On each place one slice of mozzarella cheese, one tomato slice and sprinkle on the basil. Top with the other piece of bread. Stir together the beaten egg and the milk and place in a shallow bowl. Dip sandwiches into egg mixture. Heat oil and fry sandwiches until golden brown on each side. Serve immediately. Serves 4.

Turkey Monte Cristo

In natural food stores and many supermarkets, luncheon meat without preservatives is available. Turkey meat is most frequently found, and it is very good in a variety of sandwiches, including the one below.

⅓ cup butter or
  margarine,
  softened
1½ tsp. Dijon mustard
8 slices whole
  wheat bread
4 slices Swiss
  cheese
4 slices turkey
  luncheon meat
2 eggs
¼ cup milk
  oil for frying

Beat together the butter and the mustard. Spread thinly on one side of each piece of bread. Place on top of each a slice of cheese and a slice of turkey. In a small bowl beat together the eggs and milk. Heat oil in a large skillet. Dip sandwiches into egg and milk mixture and cook until golden brown on each side. Serve immediately.
Serves 4.

Creamy Avocado Sandwiches

1   soft, ripe avocado
⅓   cup cream cheese,
    softened
    dash garlic salt
    dash oregano
    whole wheat bread
    sunflower seeds
    alfalfa sprouts
    optional: tomato
    slices

In a small bowl beat together the avocado, cream cheese, garlic salt, and oregano until fluffy. Spread on whole wheat bread. Sprinkle on the sunflower seeds and, if desired, the tomato slices. Top with alfalfa sprouts, top with another slice of bread and serve.

Sweet Brie Sandwich

Camembert cheese can be used in the place of brie if desired.

slices of brie
raisin bread
sprouts
a bit of honey

On whole wheat bread place the brie and sprouts. Drizzle a little bit of honey over. Top with another slice of bread or serve open face.

Curried Egg and Cucumber

This is a very refreshing sandwich, good for a summer lunch.

4   eggs, scrambled
1   T. green onions,
    chopped
¼   cup mayonnaise
1   tsp. curry powder
    cucumber slices
    alfalfa sprouts
    whole wheat bread

In a medium bowl combine the eggs, green onion, mayonnaise and curry powder. On whole wheat bread, layer egg mixture, cucumber slices, alfalfa sprouts. Top with another slice of whole wheat bread.

Goat Cheese in Pita

Use a mild, young goat cheese for this recipe.

slices of goat
cheese
1 tomato in chunks
½ cucumber in
chunks
lettuce or alfalfa
sprouts
4 pieces of pita
bread

Dressing:
¾ cup plain yogurt
¼ tsp. garlic powder
2 T. fresh parsley,
finely minced
dash dried mint
dash oregano

In halves of pita bread, place the goat cheese, tomato, cucumber and lettuce or alfalfa sprouts. Stir together the yogurt, garlic powder, parsley, mint and oregano. Spoon into pita and serve.

Serves 4.

Hot Pepper and Onion Sandwich

I really like this sandwich. It is very filling and hearty and reminds me of eating in an East coast deli.

¼ cup olive oil
3 green peppers,
sliced
1 onion, sliced
4 slices mozzarella
cheese
Parmesan cheese
2 large whole wheat
French rolls, cut
in half and
toasted

Preheat oven to 400°. In a medium skillet heat the olive oil. Add the green peppers and onions and saute until soft. Pile on top of halves of rolls. Top with a slice of cheese and sprinkle on Parmesan. Place in oven uncovered 5-10 minutes or until cheese melts. Serve immediately.

Serves 4.

Spinach and Onion Sandwich

hard boiled egg, sliced
fresh spinach leaves
red onion, sliced
mixture of mustard and
  mayonnaise
whole wheat bread

Spread whole wheat bread with the mixture of mustard and mayonnaise. Layer hard boiled egg slices, spinach leaves and very thin slices of red onion. Top with another slice of bread and serve.

SOUPS

*Feed your faith
and your doubts will starve to death.*

SOUPS

It may not be as quick as opening a can of soup, but making your own soup is definitely worth the additional effort. At the same time, making homemade soup doesn't take as long as some people imagine. You don't have to simmer your soup on the stove all day, soak beans for hours and make homemade stock to have good soup. You just have to have good, easy recipes—and that is what the following section is all about.

Hearty Bean and Vegetable Soup

By using canned beans instead of the dried ones that need soaking, you are able to make this hearty soup in under one hour.

2 T. oil
2 T. butter or
   margarine
2 medium onions,
   chopped
3 cloves garlic,
   crushed or minced
8 cups chicken
   broth
1 small head of
   cabbage, sliced
2 large new
   potatoes, cubed
2 cups celery, sliced
2 cups carrots,
   sliced
2 15 oz. cans of
   either Great
   Northern or Butter
   beans
1 16 oz. pkg. frozen
   corn
2 tsp. dried basil
   leaves
1 tsp. dried
   marjoram
¼ tsp. dried oregano
1 tsp. salt
½ tsp. pepper

In a large kettle place the oil and butter or margarine. Add the onions and the garlic and heat, stirring occasionally until the onions are soft and golden. Add the chicken broth, cabbage, potatoes, celery, and carrots. Bring to a boil, then turn down heat and cook for about 20 minutes or until vegetables are just barely tender. Add the beans, undrained, frozen corn and the spices. Heat through and serve.

Serves 6-8.

White Gazpacho

3 cucumbers
1 clove garlic
2 T. green onion,
   white part only,
   chopped
2 cups plain yogurt
1 cup buttermilk
2 T. lemon juice
   dash salt and
   pepper
2 tomatoes,
   chopped
4 scallions, green
   part included,
   chopped

Peel and chop cucumber. Place cucumbers, garlic, and green onion in food processor or blender. Puree. Add yogurt, buttermilk and lemon juice and combine well. If you have a small processor or are using a blender, do in several batches. Add salt and pepper to taste. Chill for about 20 minutes. Serve with tomatoes and scallions sprinkled on top.

Serves 6-8.

Curried Mushroom Soup

The curry powder really adds a zing to what can normally be a rather bland soup.

3 T. butter or
   margarine
½ onion, finely
   minced
1 clove garlic, finely
   minced
1-2 tsp. curry powder
1 cup mushrooms,
   finely chopped
6 T. flour
6 cups milk
2 tsp. dry chicken
   bouillon granules
2 T. honey
1 T. lemon juice
   lemon slices

In a soup kettle melt the butter or margarine. Add onion, garlic and curry powder and cook until onions are soft. Add flour and cook a few more minutes. Add milk and bouillon granules and stir until it thickens slightly. Add mushrooms, honey, and lemon. Heat about 10 minutes over medium heat, not allowing it to boil, and serve.

Serves 6-8.

150 SOUPS

Green Vegetables Spring Soup

1 10 oz. pkg. frozen
  asparagus pieces
1 10 oz. pkg. frozen
  green peas
1 avocado
2 green onions
8 cups milk
1 tsp. Spike (herb
  salt sold in natural
  food stores)
¼ tsp. dried
  marjoram
  pinch thyme
  pinch of dried
  mint

Run warm water over frozen vegetables until slightly thawed. Peel avocado and chop green onions. In a food processor or blender, in several batches, blend together the asparagus pieces, peas, avocado, green onions and milk. Place in a large soup kettle. Add Spike, marjoram, thyme and mint. Heat over low heat, not allowing to boil, and serve. Serves 8.

Quick Tomato Noodle Soup

Super easy and yummy.

3 T. oil
1 onion, chopped
3 carrots, sliced
3 sticks celery,
  sliced
3 cups water
2 16 oz. cans
  tomatoes,
  chopped
1 cup vegetable or
  whole wheat
  noodles
1 tsp. basil
  dash salt and
  pepper

In a large kettle place the oil, onion, carrots and celery. Cook briefly, until onion is barely soft. Add water and tomatoes, juice included, and boil 5 minutes. Add noodles, basil, salt and pepper. Cook till noodles are done. Serves 6.

Corn Chowder

3 T. butter or
  margarine
1 onion, chopped
3 sticks celery,
  chopped
1 green onion,
  chopped
3 T. flour
6 cups milk
2 tsp. chicken
  bouillon granules
1 16 oz. pkg. frozen
  corn
2 tsp. Spike (herb
  salt sold in natural
  food stores)

In the bottom of a large kettle melt the butter or margarine. Add the onion, celery, and green onion and saute a few minutes. Stir in flour and cook a few minutes. Add milk and stir constantly for a few more minutes. Add chicken bouillon granules, frozen corn and Spike. Heat, stirring occasionally until heated through. Do not allow to boil.

Serves 6.

Cauliflower Cheese Soup

3 T. butter or
  margarine
3 green onions, tops
  only, finely minced
3 T. flour
6 cups milk
1 16 oz. pkg. frozen
  cauliflower pieces
¼ cup grated
  Parmesan cheese
1 cup grated
  cheddar cheese
  dash cayenne
  pepper
  paprika

In the bottom of a large skillet saute the green onions in melted butter or margarine for a few minutes. Add flour and cook, stirring constantly for a few minutes more. Add 5 cups of the milk and stir together well. Run the cauliflower under warm water to thaw slightly. Puree 1 cup of the cauliflower pieces with the remaining one cup of milk. Place in pot. If the remaining pieces are fairly large, cut in half and add to pot. If small, add as they are. Stir in Parmesan cheese and ½ cup of the cheddar cheese. Add dash of cayenne pepper. Stir until cheese melts. Garnish each serving with remaining cheddar cheese sprinkled on top. Sprinkle paprika on top of that.

Serves 6.

Clear Mushroom Soup

Nice as a first course for a fancy company dinner.

2 T. butter or
  margarine
½ onion, chopped
2 cups mushrooms,
  sliced
2 cans consomme
  or beef broth
1 T. soy sauce
  dash Worchester-
  shire
2 green onions,
  chopped

In the bottom of a soup kettle melt the butter or margarine. Add the onions and mushrooms and saute a few minutes. Add consomme or beef broth, soy and Worchestershire, heat through. Garnish with chopped green onions and serve.

Serves 4-6.

VEGETABLES
AND
SIDE DISHES

Kind words are short to speak,
but their echoes are endless.

VEGETABLES AND SIDE DISHES

If there is one area of food that we most often lack in our diets, it is probably the area of vegetables. Visions of watery canned peas or overcooked spinach have contributed to this situation.

Properly and imaginatively cooked and seasoned vegetables can be a real taste treat in the diet as well as supplying many needed vitamins, minerals and fiber. To end up with a good product, use as few canned vegetables as possible and rely on fresh and frozen vegetables.

Though nothing beats vegetables that are freshly grown, frozen vegetables are often higher in nutritional content than vegetables that have been sitting in the supermarket for a long time. This is so because many frozen vegetables are frozen the day they are picked and their nutrients preserved while some fresh vegetables in the markets have been sitting for days, being sprayed with water which leeches out valuable nutrients.

Any meal can benefit from the addition of the recipes below. They take so little time to prepare and the nutritional benefits are so great you'll want to try them soon.

Dilled Carrots and Peas

This recipe makes a very pretty color combination.

2 T. butter or margarine 4 carrots, sliced 1 cup frozen peas ½ tsp. dill weed	In a medium skillet over medium heat melt the butter or margarine. Add the carrots and saute, stirring occasionally until barely tender, but still quite crisp. Add peas and dill, stir to combine. Cover a few minutes, and cook until peas are just heated through. Serves 4.

Italian Peas

1 pkg. frozen artichoke hearts 2 T. butter or margarine ½ onion, chopped 1 10 oz. pkg. frozen peas ¼ cup chicken broth	Run artichoke hearts under warm water to thaw slightly. Cut in half and pat dry. In a medium skillet melt the butter. Add the onion and saute a few minutes. Add the artichoke hearts and saute a few minutes. Add the frozen peas and chicken broth. Cover and heat until peas are heated through. Serves 4.

Tangy Tomato Wedges

This is a really delicious way to prepare fresh tomatoes, a good source of Vitamin C.

3 ripe tomatoes 1 clove garlic, finely minced ⅛ tsp. dried tarragon salt and pepper 1-2 T. Parmesan cheese	Preheat oven to 350°. Cut tomatoes in wedges and place in a baking dish. Sprinkle other ingredients over the top and bake uncovered about 20 minutes or until tomatoes are tender. Serves 4.

Sauteed Artichoke Hearts

This is a good side dish to serve with pasta or other Italian food.

1 box frozen
  artichoke hearts,
  thawed
  fresh lemon juice
  salt and pepper
  flour
2 T. butter or
  margarine
2 T. olive oil

Separate thawed artichoke hearts and cut in half. Sprinkle with lemon juice and salt and pepper. Dip lightly in flour. In a medium skillet over medium heat melt the butter or margarine and add the olive oil. When oil mixture is hot, put in the artichoke pieces and cook them about 5 minutes.

Serves 2-4.

 ## Red and Green Beans

This is a very hearty vegetable combination. Good for eating in the winter.

2 T. oil
½ onion, finely
  chopped
1 clove garlic,
  minced
¼ cup water
2 cups frozen green
  beans
1 16 oz. can red
  kidney beans
¼ tsp. thyme

In a medium saucepan over medium heat saute the onions and garlic in the oil until the onion is soft. Add the water, green beans, kidney beans and thyme. Cover and cook until heated through.

Serves 4.

 ## Cranberry Apples

This is a wonderful side dish to serve with any of the chicken or turkey entrees. It is especially nice for the holidays.

Cranberry Apples, continued.

4 medium size tart
  apples
½ cup lemon juice
⅓ cup water
½ teaspoon salt
2 cups fresh or
  frozen cranberries
½ cup water
⅓ cup honey
¼ cup walnuts or
  pecans, chopped
1 T. butter
¼ tsp. cinnamon
½ tsp. lemon peel

Cut in half and core the apples. Place in mixture of lemon juice, water and salt. Cover and steam for 15-20 minutes until tender, but not mushy. While the apples are cooking, place the cranberries and water in a medium size saucepan. Cook until the cranberries burst. Allow water to cook away. Then add honey, chopped walnuts or pecans, butter, cinnamon and lemon peel. Heat through and stir to combine nuts and spices.

Remove apples from liquid, place in oven-proof dish. Top with cranberry mixture. The apples can be used immediately as a garnish, or covered and reheated later.

Serves 6-8.

Squash and Tomato Medley

2 zucchini squash,
  thinly sliced
2 yellow squash,
  thinly sliced
2 tomatoes, thinly
  sliced
  olive oil
½ tsp. basil
  salt and pepper

Preheat oven to 400°. In a 9 x 13 glass baking dish arrange the slices of vegetables in rows, alternating different vegetables. Brush with olive oil, sprinkle on basil, salt and pepper. Cover and bake about 20 minutes.

Serves 4.

Broccoli Almondine

2 cups frozen
  broccoli pieces
2 T. soy sauce
2 T. butter or
  margarine
2 tsp. lemon juice
1 tsp. honey
½ cup sliced
  almonds

Cook broccoli pieces with a little water over medium heat until just barely heated through. While broccoli is cooking combine the soy sauce, butter or margarine, lemon juice, honey and almonds in small saucepan. Cook for a few minutes. Pour over broccoli and stir to combine.

Serves 4.

Stir-Fried Peas and Celery

This is especially good served with an oriental dinner though it tastes great with other meals also.

2 T. oil
3 stalks celery,
 sliced thinly
2 cups frozen green
 peas
1 pkg. frozen snow
 peas
¼ cup chicken broth
1 tsp. honey

In a wok or skillet add the oil and saute the celery a minute or two. Add frozen peas and snow peas. Stir together chicken broth and honey. Pour over mixture and cover. Heat a few minutes until peas are thawed.
 Serves 4-6.

Variation: A small can of water chestnuts, sliced, can also be added.

Broccoli with Garlic Lemon Sauce

1 16 oz. pkg. frozen
 broccoli
2 T. butter or
 margarine
½ cup onions, diced
2 cloves garlic,
 finely minced
2 T. fresh lemon
 juice
1 T. fresh parsley,
 chopped
½ tsp. basil

Prepare frozen broccoli according to package directions. In a small skillet melt the butter or margarine. Add the onions and garlic and saute until onion is soft. Add lemon juice, parsley, and basil. Stir together a few minutes. Pour over cooked broccoli and serve.
 Serves 8.

Variations: This sauce is also good over asparagus and green beans.

Creamy Mushrooms

Rather rich, these are good with a very plain entree.

Creamy Mushrooms, continued.

3 T. butter or
   margarine
2 cups fresh
   mushrooms, cut in
   half
3 green onions,
   sliced
⅓ cup plain yogurt

In a small skillet melt the butter or margarine. Add the mushrooms and onions and saute briefly until mushrooms are tender. Gently stir in yogurt, heat through and serve.
Serves 4.

Chili Limas

I prefer the baby limas in this recipe, but the regular size can also be used.

1 10 oz. pkg. frozen
   lima beans
2 T. chopped chili
   peppers
¼ tsp. chili powder
½ cup plain yogurt
   or sour cream

Cook frozen limas according to package directions. Stir in chili peppers, chili powder and yogurt or sour cream. Heat through and serve.
Serves 4.

Sauteed Okra and Tomatoes

1 10 oz. pkg. frozen
   okra
2 T. butter or
   margarine
¼ cup onions,
   chopped
1 16 oz. can
   tomatoes, drained
   or 4 fresh
   tomatoes, cut in
   wedges
   optional: ½ tsp.
   gumbo file

Thaw okra. In a medium skillet melt the butter or margarine. Add the onions and saute briefly. Add the tomatoes and the gumbo file. Cover and cook over low heat until heated through.
Serves 4.

VEGETARIAN MAIN DISHES

Take time to work—it is the price of success;
Take time to think—it is the source of power;
Take time to play—it is the secret of perpetual youth;
Take time to read—it is the foundation of wisdom;
Take time to worship—it is the highway to reverence;
Take time to be friendly—it is the road to happiness;
Take time to dream—it is hitching our wagon to a star;
Take time to love and be loved—it is a gift of God.
                                                    —Anonymous

VEGETARIAN MAIN DISHES

In the interests of health and budget, it's a good idea to include some vegetarian main dishes in your weekly meal planning. Unfortunately many people fear that healthful, vegetarian main dishes are difficult to prepare or boring in taste. Nothing could be further from the truth as the dishes below illustrate. Each dish is so delicious and filling no one will even think about asking where the meat is and, of course, none of them take more than an hour to prepare.

To complete a meal with any of the main dishes below, a tossed salad and homemade bread are perfect.

Vegetarian Stroganoff

Yummy and creamy, just like the version made with beef, but much less expensive to make.

1 **16 oz. frozen broccoli and cauliflower pieces**
2 **T. oil**
1 **large onion, chopped**
2 **cups fresh mushrooms, cut in half**
½ **cup beef bouillon**
⅛ **tsp. dill**
¼ **tsp. paprika**
  dash salt and pepper
½ **cup sour cream**
½ **cup yogurt**
4 **cups cooked whole wheat noodles**

Cook broccoli and cauliflower pieces according to package directions. While they are cooking, place the oil in a large skillet and heat over medium heat. Add chopped onion and mushrooms and cook until tender. Add beef bouillon, dill, paprika, salt and pepper. Add cooked vegetables and simmer 5 minutes. Stir in sour cream and yogurt, heat through and serve over whole wheat noodles.
Serves 6.

Green Chili Rice

2 T. butter or
margarine
1 cup chopped
onion
⅓ cup chopped
celery
5 cups cooked
brown rice
1 cup cottage
cheese
1 cup plain yogurt
½ cup milk
1 4 oz. can chopped
green chili
peppers
dash salt and
pepper
1 cup shredded
cheddar cheese

In a small saucepan over medium heat melt the butter or margarine. Add the chopped onions and celery and cook until tender. In a 9 × 13 casserole stir together the cooked celery and onion, brown rice, cottage cheese, yogurt, chili peppers, salt and pepper and ½ of the cheddar cheese. Sprinkle the rest of the cheddar cheese on top. Bake in a 350° oven 30 minutes and serve.

Serves 6-8.

Mexican Casserole

This is absolutely delicious, one of my all time favorite Mexican dishes.

3 T. oil
1 onion, chopped
2 cloves garlic,
minced
4 fresh tomatoes,
chopped
2 oz. green chili
peppers, chopped
dash of salt
12 corn tortillas
2 cups jack cheese,
grated
½ cup sour cream
paprika

Preheat oven to 350°. Place the oil in a large skillet and saute the onions and garlic until the onions are soft. Add the tomatoes, chili peppers and a dash of salt. Saute 5 more minutes. Cut tortillas into quarters. In a 1½-2 quart casserole make alternate layers of the tortillas, tomato mixture and cheese until all ingredients are used. Bake about 30 minutes or until heated through. Top with sour cream. Sprinkle with paprika and serve.

Serves 4.

Vegetables with Spicy Peanut Sauce

This is my version of the Indonesian dish Gado Gado which is basically a combination of beans, vegetables and grains topped with a very spicy peanut-flavored sauce. It's different and delicious.

1 16 oz. pkg. frozen, fancy vegetables (such as Italian or Florentine), cooked according to package directions
3 cups cooked brown rice
  Spicy Peanut Sauce (recipe below)
½ cup peanuts, chopped

Sauce:
2 T. oil
1 medium onion, chopped
2 cloves garlic, mashed
1 cup crunchy peanut butter
2 cups water
3 T. lemon juice
1 tsp. soy sauce
1 T. honey
½ tsp. cayenne pepper, or to taste
½ tsp. salt

To make the sauce, heat oil in a large skillet over low heat. Add onion and garlic and cook until onion is soft, stirring occasionally. Stir in peanut butter, water and lemon juice until well combined. Stir in soy sauce, honey, cayenne and salt. Simmer over low heat for 10 minutes, stirring occasionally.

On a large platter spread out the brown rice. Top with the cooked vegetables. Spread Spicy Peanut Sauce on top, sprinkle with peanuts and serve.

Serves 6.

Bean Tamale Pie

3 T. oil
½ cup onion, chopped
¼ cup green pepper, chopped
2 cloves garlic, minced
1 15 oz. can cooked kidney beans
2 cup frozen whole kernel corn
1 16 oz. can tomatoes, chopped
1 6 oz. can tomato paste
2 tsp. chili powder
½ tsp. cumin
dash salt
⅔ cup cornmeal
1⅓ cups water
dash salt
chili powder

Place the oil in a medium skillet and saute the onion, garlic and green pepper about 5 minutes. Add beans, corn, tomato paste, spices and cook for 10 minutes. While cooking, mix together cornmeal, water and salt, and cook over low heat, stirring constantly till mixture becomes thick. Pour bean mixture into a 3 quart baking dish. Spread cornmeal mixture on top. Sprinkle on chili powder and bake in a 350° oven until hot and bubbly around the edges, about 30 minutes.

Serves 6-8.

Vegetarian Eggs Fu-Yung

Eggs Fu-Yung are basically little egg-vegetable pancakes. In place of the vegetables given below, you can also use an equal amount of any variety of leftover vegetables.

Sauce:
- 1 **cup chicken broth**
- 3 **T. soy sauce**
- ½ **tsp. Chinese Five Spice**
- 1 **T. cornstarch**
- ¼ **cup water**

Egg mixture:
- 2 **T. oil**
- ⅓ **cup green onions**
- ½ **cup zucchini, chopped**
- 1 **cup fresh mushrooms, chopped**
- 2 **cups fresh bean sprouts**
- 7 **eggs**
- 3 **T. oil**

In a small pan heat together the chicken broth, soy sauce and Chinese Five Spice. Dissolve cornstarch in water. Add to mixture and cook, stirring constantly until mixture thickens and boils. Turn down heat, but keep warm, while making egg patties.

In a medium skillet place the oil. Saute onions and zucchini a few minutes and then add mushrooms and bean sprouts. Saute until all vegetables are tender. In a medium bowl beat eggs until fluffy and light. Add cooked vegetables to egg mixture. Stir together. Heat oil in a large skillet over medium heat. Place about ½ cupsful of vegetable and egg mixture into skillet to make patties. Cook until lightly browned on one side, turn over and brown on the other side. Serve topped with sauce.

Serves 6.

Bean Sprout Sukiyaki

When you stir-fry vegetables, it is one of the most healthful ways you can prepare them because the high heat seals in the nutrients. Also, you always want your stir-fried vegetables to be somewhat crisp and this prevents you from overcooking them.

3 T. oil
2 cups tofu, cut in
   chunks
3 T. soy sauce
¼ cup chicken
   bouillon
1 tsp. Chinese Five
   Spice
1 cup celery, sliced
½ cup carrots, sliced
1 cup Chinese
   cabbage, sliced
1 cup fresh bean
   sprouts
½ cup green onions
1 cup fresh spinach,
   chopped

In a wok or frying pan, heat the oil. Add tofu and cook a few minutes. Add soy sauce. Stir together chicken bouillon and Chinese Five Spice. Add to pan. Add celery, carrots, Chinese cabbage, green onions and bean sprouts. Cover and steam for 10 minutes. Add spinach. Cook covered for about 3 more minutes. Stir together and serve over brown rice or ramen.

Serves 6.

Cheese and Bean Enchiladas

The topping of sour cream, avocado, and green onion over the hot enchiladas makes this a very special Mexican food dish.

Sauce:
- 2 T. oil
- 1 medium onion, chopped
- 2 T. flour
- 1½ cups chicken broth
- 1 16 oz. can tomatoes
- 1 4 oz. can chopped mild green chilis

Filling:
- 12 corn tortillas
- 1 16 oz. can refried beans
- 4 cups cheddar cheese

Topping:
- 1 avocado, sliced
- 1 cup sour cream
- ¼ cup green onion, chopped

In a medium skillet saute the onion and garlic till soft. Add the flour and cook for a minute. In a blender or food processor puree the chicken broth and the tomatoes together. Add this mixture to the skillet and cook a few minutes. Add chilis and simmer about 7 minutes. Dip each tortilla in sauce. Place some refried beans, cheese and a spoonful of sauce in each. Roll up and place in a baking dish. Top enchiladas with remaining sauce. Bake uncovered for 15 minutes at 350°. Remove from oven, top with avocado, sour cream and green onions. Serve immediately. Serves 6.

A house is made of walls and beams;
a home is built with love and dreams.

Index
of Recipes